BEYOND
PREEMPTION

BEYOND PREEMPTION

FORCE AND LEGITIMACY IN A CHANGING WORLD

IVO H. DAALDER

editor

BROOKINGS INSTITUTION PRESS
Washington, D.C.

Copyright © 2007
THE BROOKINGS INSTITUTION
1775 Massachusetts Avenue, N.W., Washington, D.C. 20036
www.brookings.edu

Library of Congress Cataloging-in-Publication data

Beyond preemption : force and legitimacy in a changing world / Ivo H. Daalder, editor.
  p. cm.
  Summary: "Makes proposals for how to forge a new international consensus on the use
of force, including its preemptive use, to address today's interrelated threats of terrorism,
weapons of mass destruction, and humanitarian crises. Considers how these strategies
could be best legitimized and made palatable to domestic and international
communities"—Provided by publisher.
  Includes bibliographical references and index.
  ISBN-13: 978-0-8157-1685-3 (pbk. : alk. paper)
  ISBN-10: 0-8157-1685-0 (pbk. : alk. paper)
  1. Intervention (International law) 2. Security, International. 3. Humanitarian
intervention. 4. War (International law) 5. National security—United States. 6. United
States—Military policy. I. Daalder, Ivo H.
  JZ6368.B45 2007
  327.1'17—dc22   2007015792

9 8 7 6 5 4 3 2 1

The paper used in this publication meets minimum requirements of the
American National Standard for Information Sciences—Permanence of Paper
for Printed Library Materials: ANSI Z39.48-1992.

Typeset in Sabon with Baker Signet display

Composition by Cynthia Stock
Silver Spring, Maryland

Printed by R. R. Donnelley
Harrisonburg, Virginia

Contents

Foreword

THE DECISION ON whether, when, and how to use military force is the most consequential a nation's leaders can make. It is also, properly, a national decision—one of the most essential prerogatives of sovereignty. But as Americans and the world have been reminded in recent years, if a national decision is made without sufficient regard to whether its use of force has legitimacy in the eyes of the international community, the result can be a setback to the cause of peace and to the interests of the nation that has gone to war.

The administration of President George W. Bush has provided two contrasting examples illustrating this principle. Operation Enduring Freedom, which brought down the Taliban regime in Afghanistan after 9/11, had widespread support around the world. It might have laid the ground for a sustainable success had the administration not quickly turned its attention and its resources to toppling the regime of Saddam Hussein. Operation Iraqi Freedom has gone badly in large measure because it did not have legitimacy in the eyes of the world. There are other reasons as well, including a cascade of mistakes in the way the occupation was conceived and executed. But at the core of the whole episode was a decision in Washington to use force in defiance of the United Nations Security Council and over the objections of a number of America's best friends and staunchest allies.

If every nation decided solely on its own when and how to use force, anarchy would prevail—and the use of force might again, as in the past, become part of the natural order of things. Indeed, as this timely and cogent book makes clear, one of the most important developments of the past sixty years has been the emerging global consensus that using force is *not* part of the natural order of things. Its use, at least as a means to resolve interstate differences, has become an extraordinary development. One reason for this change is that in the wake of history's most destructive conflict—World War II—the world adopted specific rules on the use of force. They can be found in the UN Charter, which explicitly prohibits the use of force in interstate relations and recognizes only two exceptions: when nations must defend themselves and when they have the authorization of the UN Security Council.

Since 1945 states have generally lived up to these rules, at least in spirit. While the United States has resorted to military action frequently since 1945, it has always justified its use on the basis of an internationally agreed framework—that is either as an instance of individual or collective self-defense or on the basis of a Security Council authorization. The Kennedy, Johnson, and Nixon administrations all justified the Vietnam War on the grounds that they were helping the South defend itself against the North; after the Gulf of Tonkin incident, the United States claimed self-defense on its own behalf. The administration of George H. W. Bush took the position that in launching the first Gulf War it was engaged in collective self-defense, and it had the backing of the UN to use "all necessary means" to oust Saddam's occupation forces from Kuwait. Similarly, the Clinton administration had the support of the Security Council to lead NATO's intervention in Bosnia. In the trickier case of Kosovo, the Russians blocked a consensus in the Security Council, but Kofi Annan provided a kind of bridging justification for the bombing of Serbia in his capacity as secretary general while the United States and the European Union collaborated with Russia on the diplomacy to end the war. However, the current administration, in launching the second Gulf War, took the self-defense argument a big step further by arguing that it could use force even when the threat was not clearly imminent or clearly directed at the United States itself. Or, as the title of this book puts it, President Bush went "beyond preemption."

That development—the consequences of which will be with America and the world well beyond the Bush presidency—has been another in a series of setbacks for the post–World War II international system. With the end of the cold war, it has become increasingly apparent that conditions within individual states are at least as likely to pose a threat to international peace and stability as cross-border aggression. This has proved true in a number of different circumstances. In the case of dictatorial states, massive human rights violations have created civil conflicts that spill over borders through large-scale refugee flows (for example, Iraqi Kurds who poured over the borders into Iran and Syria in the early nineties and the ethnic Albanians who fled Kosovo into Macedonia at the end of that decade) and cross-border civil conflicts erupting among neighbors with ethnically homologous populations (for example, Congo and the broader Great Lakes region of Africa, as well as Afghanistan and its neighbors). Failed states also pose a threat to peace and security as havens for terrorists and international criminal organizations, drug and human traffickers, and spillover civil conflicts (for example, Ethiopia and Somalia).

The spread of weapons of mass destruction has posed a particularly severe challenge to the international system. The mere possession of WMD by a growing number of states increases the likelihood that the norms against the use of WMD will be eroded, a major threat to international peace and security. This is especially true as dangerous, authoritarian, or unstable states acquire WMD capability. That sort of proliferation increases the chances that these weapons will be used or that terrorists will acquire WMD capabilities.

In addition to questions about the adequacy of international principles intended to regulate the use of force, the effectiveness of the institutional mechanisms designed to implement them has also come under growing pressure. With the end of the cold war, there was hope that the Security Council might finally assume its intended role as the principal instrument for authorizing force, and during the early 1990s, the number of UN missions expanded dramatically. The UN's slow response to violence in Bosnia and its failure in Somalia and Rwanda were due as much to the decisions of member states as to the organization itself. Nonetheless, those episodes underscored why the Security Council should not be the ultimate arbiter in deciding whether to use force to meet humanitarian emergencies arising out of actions by a state against its own people.

Dealing with WMD requires effective measures for enforcement, and here again, the Security Council has proved a highly imperfect instrument. For twelve years, it struggled—and sometimes tied itself in knots—over how to enforce the disarmament resolutions enacted after the 1991 Gulf War. A similar hesitancy has marked the response to North Korea's and Iran's violations of their nonproliferation commitments.

It is against the backdrop of this history and this challenge to the efficacy of the international system that the Brookings Institution, in 2003, launched a major project on "Force and Legitimacy in the Evolving International System." Led by then vice president of foreign policy studies James Steinberg and by senior fellow Ivo Daalder, a team of American strategists, analysts, and international lawyers engaged in a series of bilateral workshops and dialogues with counterparts from around the world. Its regular participants included Bruce Jentleson (Duke University), Edward Luck (Columbia University), Susan Rice (Brookings), David Scheffer (Northwestern University), Anne-Marie Slaughter (Princeton University), Walter Slocombe (Caplin and Drysdale), and Paul Stares (U.S. Institute of Peace).

Over the course of nearly three years, the Brookings-led team worked with government officials, scholars, and legal and military experts from Europe, Russia, China, Mexico and Latin America, South Asia, the Middle East, and sub-Saharan Africa. In October 2006 Brookings brought together many of these participants in Washington for two days of extended discussion on what had been learned and how to move forward.

The chapters in this volume originated as short discussion papers for this international conference. Ivo Daalder provides an overview of the recent debate over the use of force and proposes ways in which the existing framework might be adapted to new realities. James Steinberg, Bruce Jentleson, and Susan Rice and Andrew Loomis discuss the role of force in dealing with weapons of mass destruction, terrorism, and grave humanitarian emergencies, respectively. Anne Kramer summarizes the project's workshop and conference discussions.

The Brookings Project on Force and Legitimacy in the Evolving International System was made possible by the generous support of the

Carnegie Corporation New York, the European Commission of the European Union, the William and Flora Hewlett Foundation, the John D. and Catherine D. MacArthur Foundation, and the Rockefeller Brothers Fund.

All of us at Brookings are proud to be associated with the project and with this book.

STROBE TALBOTT
President

Washington, D.C.
May 2007

BEYOND
PREEMPTION

CHAPTER ONE

Beyond Preemption: An Overview

Ivo H. Daalder

THE ISSUES OF force and legitimacy—of when to use military force, for what purpose, and who should decide—became highly contentious internationally as a result of three developments: the Kosovo campaign of 1999, the terrorist attacks of September 2001, and the Iraq war of 2003. Each of these events raised difficult questions about the continued applicability of the international framework governing the use of force. That framework, enshrined in the United Nations Charter signed at the end of the Second World War, was designed with one principal purpose in mind: to avoid another interstate conflict as devastating and destructive as the one that had just ended. Accordingly, the UN Charter proscribed "the threat or use of force against the territorial integrity or political independence of any state" (Article 2[4]). It recognized only two exceptions to this prohibition: "the inherent right of individual and collective right of self-defense if an armed attack occurs" (Article 51), and any use of force authorized by the UN Security Council in order "to maintain or restore international peace and security" (Article 42).

The Kosovo campaign, in which nineteen NATO countries launched a seventy-eight-day air war to halt Serbian efforts to oust the Albanian population of Kosovo from the country, met neither exception to the prohibition of the use of force. It was not an instance of self-defense, since the people being defended were citizens of the very state that was being attacked. Furthermore, the NATO action was not directly authorized by the Security Council, since at least one permanent member (Russia) had made clear that it would veto any resolution authorizing the use of force in this instance. The terrorist attacks on the Twin Towers and the Pentagon of September 2001 raised to prominence the threat posed by nonstate actors and the issue of how to respond to such an attack. The Iraq war raised the question of whether explicit Security Council authorization was necessary to enforce its resolutions and, importantly, who decides whether this is necessary or not.

To address these questions and seek answers that might gain agreement from a wide range of actors around the world, the Brookings Institution in 2003 launched a major project on "Force and Legitimacy in the Evolving International System." The project consisted of a series of workshops with officials, scholars, and legal and military experts from Europe, Russia, China, Latin America, South Asia, the Middle East, and sub-Saharan Africa. The workshops and a final international conference engaged in wide-ranging discussions of whether and when force might be used and how its use could best be legitimized. This volume builds on these discussions and proposes ways in which a renewed international consensus on these crucial issues might be forged.

The workshop and conference discussions during these three years, which are examined in greater detail by Anne Kramer in the final chapter of this volume, proved to be rich and rewarding, sometimes surprising, and always stimulating. In each session participants examined the appropriateness of using force in dealing with weapons of mass destruction, terrorism, and humanitarian crises, as well as ways (institutional and otherwise) such uses of force could best be legitimized. What follows are some of the project's key findings.

First, there was widespread agreement that force—even when used preemptively—can be an appropriate response to the terrorist threat. Of course, defining what constitutes such a threat is not easy, as discussions of this issue at the United Nations have long underscored. Agreement to deal aggressively with terrorism was particularly strong in Russia, where discussions were held just weeks after the terrorist attack on the elementary school in Beslan that killed more than 300 people. Discussions with South Asians revealed an interesting paradox: while the use of force to confront a terrorist threat (whether preventive, preemptive, or retaliatory) now enjoys widespread legitimacy, its efficacy is increasingly in doubt.

Second, Europeans and Africans, along with Americans, believed that using force to prevent or end widespread humanitarian abuses was appropriate and, when undertaken early enough, likely to be effective. There was strong support for the notion that states have a responsibility to protect their citizens and that their failure to do so puts the onus on the international community to step in and protect these people accordingly. There was no such support for humanitarian intervention among Mexicans, South Asians, or Russians, who regarded the responsibility to protect as an unwarranted interference in the internal affairs of states. However, there were several South Asians who held that if intervention could be justified on the basis of international humanitarian law, states could act on such a basis without prior Security Council authorization provided that they report their actions to the council along with an assessment of the legal grounds for such action. Interestingly, discussions with Chinese scholars demonstrated movement from a stance of strict noninterference toward a more pragmatic evaluation of China's strategic interests—including a belief that China would have supported military intervention in Kosovo if the issue had arisen in 2006 rather than in 1999. The official Chinese view, however, remains distinctly wary of any such interventions.

Third, there was no agreement—even among Americans and Europeans—on how to respond to the proliferation of weapons of mass destruction. Even when the discussion underscored the dire consequences of countries like Iran acquiring nuclear weapons, it was impossible to gain agreement on the need for preemptive action (let alone preventive war). Here, the consequences of the disagreement over Iraq clearly had their most profound implication. Again, interestingly, China's position appears to be evolving from a principled opposition to pragmatic considerations concerning the specificity of the threat, as determined not by whether a country acquires weapons but whether its past behavior suggests their possible use. Chinese participants indicated, for example, that in 2003 Beijing likely would have supported military strikes against Iraq on the scale of the 1998 Operation Desert Fox.

Fourth, most non-Americans, including Europeans, South Asians, and the Chinese, embraced a procedural form of legitimacy, insisting that the UN Security Council is the main, if not only, international body able to authorize the use of force in situations other than self-defense. There was some sympathy for the notion that regional organizations might be able to step in if the UN Security Council would not, but this was still very much seen as a second-best option. There was no willingness to embrace the notion of substantive legitimacy—the idea that the positive outcome of the use of force might itself legitimize its use. Of course, the Kosovo intervention was partly legitimized in this way (and this paved the way to procedural legitimation after the fact). One could not help but wonder during the discussions whether sentiment might have been different if weapons of mass destruction had been discovered in Iraq.

These discussions coincided with the heated international debate that followed the Bush administration's reinterpretation of the framework guiding questions of force and legitimacy and its subsequent decision to invade Iraq. Many of those participating in the meetings were actively involved in the debate, and some helped prepare the report of the High-Level Panel on Threats, Challenges and Change, a panel that UN secretary general Kofi Annan appointed just as the Brookings project got under way. Our discussions and the search for a renewed international consensus on these important issues were therefore very much informed by the UN efforts—and vice versa.

This chapter, however, presents a view of this debate, including its merits and demerits, of one person alone. The conclusions reached and suggestions made are solely my own. They are offered in the hope that others might find them an acceptable way forward.

From Response to Prevention

The scale of destruction caused by the September 11 attacks raised the immediate and important question of how best to prevent another catastrophic event in the future—be it a terrorist attack, use of weapons of mass destruction, or a combination of the two. For the Bush administration as well as others, the answer was to act before another threat could materialize. "I will not wait on events, while dangers gather," President George W. Bush declared in January 2002. "I will not stand by, as peril draws closer and closer. The United States of America will not permit the world's most dangerous regimes to threaten us with the world's most destructive weapons."[1]

While Bush did not explain how the United States would counter this rising danger, it was evident that the administration believed preventive military force would have to be at the core of any successful strategy. This belief rested on two central arguments. First, the key actors that threatened America (rogue states and terrorists) were fundamentally different from the traditional adversaries the United States had long confronted. Whereas strategies of deterrence and containment were appropriate for dealing with the Soviet Union, they would be ineffective in confronting these new threats. "Deterrence," Bush explained, "means nothing against shadowy terrorist networks with no nation or citizens to defend. Containment is not possible when unbalanced dictators with weapons of mass destruction can deliver those weapons on missiles or secretly provide them to terrorist allies." In this new security environment, safety could no longer be assured by the ability to defeat threats after they had formed. "If we wait for threats to fully materialize, we will have waited too long."[2]

The second reason for relying on preventive force was the catastrophic cost of misjudging the imminence of the threat. "We don't want the smoking gun to be a mushroom cloud," Condoleezza Rice, Bush's national security adviser, famously declared with reference to Iraq.[3] Whatever the costs of lowering the barrier to using force preventively, the administration argued, they were outweighed by the dangers of waiting too long to act. As the National Security Strategy put it, "the greater the threat, the greater is the risk of inaction—and the more compelling the case for taking anticipatory action to defend ourselves, even if the uncertainty remains as to the time and place of the enemies' attack. To forestall or prevent such hostile acts by our adversaries, the United States will, if necessary, act preemptively."[4]

The United States was not alone in believing that the changing nature of the threat and the costly consequences of miscalculating it required countries to act preventively. Most of the major powers in the world arrived at a similar view. "Containment will not work in the face of the global threat that confronts us," explained British Prime Minister Tony Blair in 2004. "The terrorists have no intention of being contained. The states that proliferate or acquire [weapons of mass destruction] illegally are doing so precisely to avoid containment." Not every threat required military action. "But we surely have a duty and a right to prevent the threat [from] materializing," Blair insisted. "Otherwise, we are powerless to fight the aggression and injustice which over time puts at risk our security and way of life."[5] Similarly, the French government, in a defense white paper released days before the U.S. National Security Strategy was issued, maintained that

> we must be able to identify and prevent threats as soon as possible. Within this framework, possible preemptive action is not out of the question, where an explicit and confirmed threat has been recognized. This determination and the improvement of long range strike capabilities should constitute a deterrent threat for our potential aggressors, especially as transnational terrorist networks develop and organize outside our territory, in areas not governed by states, and even at times with the help of enemy states.[6]

Meanwhile, President Vladimir Putin insisted in 2003 that Russia "retains the right to launch a preemptive strike."[7] Defense Minister Sergei Ivanov later elaborated:

> The primary task for the armed forces is to prevent conventional and nuclear aggression against Russia. Hence our firm commitment to the principle of pre-emption. We define pre-emption not only as a capability to deliver strikes on terrorist groups but as other measures designed to prevent a threat from emerging long before there is a need to confront it. This is the guiding principle of the profound and comprehensive modernization of our armed forces."[8]

More recently, even a country like Japan has embraced the notion of preemption. "If we accept that there is no other option to prevent a missile attack," then chief cabinet secretary (and now prime minister) Shinzo Abe said in reference to North Korea's missile capabilities, "there is an argument that attacking the missile bases would be within the legal right of self-defense."[9]

The UN Response

The emerging sense that preemptive military action was increasingly justified by the changing nature of the threats confronting the United States and other countries was cause for deep disquiet, not least within the

United Nations. "Since this Organisation was founded," UN secretary general Kofi Annan told the General Assembly in September 2003, "States have generally sought to deal with threats to the peace through containment and deterrence, by a system based on collective security and the United Nations Charter." While states of course retained the right of self-defense when attacked, "until now it has been understood that when States go beyond that, and decide to use force to deal with broader threats to international peace and security, they need the unique legitimacy provided by the United Nations." The preemption doctrine thus represented "a fundamental challenge to the principles on which, however imperfectly, world peace and stability have rested for the last fifty-eight years. My concern is that, if it were to be adopted, it could set precedents that resulted in a proliferation of the unilateral and lawless use of force, with or without justification."[10]

The real question this development raised for Annan, however, was less whether certain states were willing to live up to this precept than whether the rules governing the use of force developed in the wake of World War II were still applicable in today's world of very different, global threats. The UN secretary general appointed a high-level panel of former statesmen (including Brent Scowcroft, Qian Qinchen, Yevgeny Primakov, and Gareth Evans) to answer this and related questions.

The December 2004 report issued by the High-Level Panel on Threats, Challenges and Change revealed an important evolution of thought on the critical question of whether and when to use force. On the question of whether the right to self-defense included a state's right to use force preemptively when faced with an imminent attack, the panel argued that it does. As to threats that are not imminent but are—like terrorism and weapons proliferation—grave and perhaps growing, the panel concluded that "if there are good arguments for preventive military action, with good evidence to support them, they should be put to the Security Council, which can authorize such action." Indeed, the panel argued that the Security Council could authorize force against a state as long as it believed such action to be necessary for maintaining or restoring international peace and security. This would be the case "whether the threat is occurring now, in the imminent future or more distant future; whether it involves the State's own actions or those of non-State actors it harbours or supports; or whether it takes the form of an act or omission, an actual or potential act of violence or simply a challenge to the Council's authority." Yet, while arguing that there are a broad range of circumstances under which force might be used, the panel declined to endorse the Bush administration's claim that under any of these circumstances states could act on their own. That, it argued, was a recipe for international anarchy rather than international order. "Allowing one to so act is to allow all."[11]

The panel's views were broadly endorsed by Kofi Annan.[12] However, two critical issues were left unresolved. One is the issue of imminence. Both the High-Level Panel and the secretary general maintained the distinction between threats that are imminent, which states have the right to address themselves under Article 51, and threats that are not imminent or latent, against which force can be used preventively only if the Security Council so authorizes. This assumes that the distinction between imminent and latent threats, which applied at a time when armed attacks required the mobilization of mass armies, is still a useful one. But is it? In a globalized world threatened by weapons of mass destruction and terrorists with global reach, this distinction loses much of its strategic meaning. Once a country has acquired weapons of mass destruction, it can decide to use them with little or no warning, either by sending them aloft on a long-range missile or handing them to terrorists to use at a time and place of their own choosing. That is, the very possession of weapons of mass destruction by some countries can pose an existential threat, whether or not their actual use is truly imminent. It follows that as long as the threats states face are unconventional (including from weapons of mass destruction and terrorism), relying on the conventional distinction between imminent and latent threats makes little sense.

The second issue left unresolved by the High-Level Panel is what to do if the Security Council fails to authorize preventive action when some states believe this is necessary to deal with a mounting threat. This is not a theoretical possibility. As the High-Level Panel acknowledged, "the Council's decisions have often been less than consistent, less than persuasive and less than fully responsive to very real state and human security needs."[13] It acted late in the case of the former Yugoslavia, ineffectively in response to Darfur, and not at all during the genocide in Rwanda. It refused to take up the matter of North Korea's noncompliance with the nuclear Non-Proliferation Treaty (NPT) until after Pyongyang actually tested a nuclear device, and it has been slow and ineffective in responding to Iran's violation of its NPT obligations. Indeed, there is a long and growing list of Security Council failures to act promptly and forcefully to maintain or restore peace and security around the world.

Unfortunately, the various proposals by the High-Level Panel and secretary general to make the Security Council a more effective and responsive body are not likely do so. Even if it were possible to reach agreement on changing and enlarging the composition of the council (which, evidently, it is not), adding more members to the council will only further impede its ability to reach consensus because of the larger number of diverse views. It is useful to set guidelines for deciding whether to authorize force—including criteria derived from the just war tradition, such as the seriousness of the threat, the purpose of the proposed action, the plausible success of alternative means to defeat the threat, the proportionality of the military response, and the likelihood of success.[14] However, their adoption by the Security Council, as Annan has urged, is unlikely to change matters much since key members will continue to perceive threats to international security in different ways. For example, a country like the United States, which has global responsibilities and interests, will view new security challenges as more serious threats to international security than would those countries that have narrower interests and responsibilities.

The same differences, moreover, will apply to judging the applicability of new guidelines to specific cases. Thus proposals to reform Security Council membership and practices will have little impact. While it would be helpful to have agreement on normative standards, the ultimate determinant of Security Council action or inaction will always be the political decisionmaking processes in differently minded and differently situated countries.

Sovereignty and State Responsibility

These difficulties point to a more fundamental problem with the existing UN Charter–based rules governing the use of force. These rules are grounded in two key principles that were the product of a particular era characterized by the end of World War II and the start of decolonization: first, states are sovereign equals, and second, states should not interfere in each other's internal affairs. Changes in the international environment during the past six decades have eroded the continued applicability of these principles, and thus the rules based on them have become much less tenable.

With regard to the first principle, sovereignty is being eroded both from within states and from without. Many states are too weak to control what happens within their own borders, with consequences that can be dire for all. "Weak states," the Bush administration rightly argued, "can pose as great a danger to our national interests as strong states."[15] In addition, rapidly increasing globalization challenges the ability of states to control their own frontiers, so developments almost anywhere on earth can pose imminent dangers almost anywhere around the globe. That, after all, is what September 11 was all about. Finally, key actors on the world stage—terrorists, nuclear technology traffickers, international criminal cartels, multinational corporations, and nongovernmental organizations—are powerful and purposeful but decidedly *not* sovereign.

There is, in short, much more to international relations than the interaction of sovereign states. That is a profound change from the world of 1945, with many significant implications, not least the changing nature of the threats and the role of force in dealing with them. The main threat today is no longer the external behavior of states but rather the external consequences of their internal behavior. Just consider, the last three wars the United States has fought were in response to how particular states behaved regarding matters within their borders. The Kosovo war was about protecting the Albanian minority from ethnic cleansing by Serb forces. The Afghanistan war was about the Taliban providing a sanctuary to al Qaeda and Osama bin Laden. And the Iraq war was about the purported development of weapons of mass destruction by Saddam Hussein's regime.

The UN system was not set up to deal with these types of threats, given that it stresses both the sovereign equality of states and the principle of noninterference in their internal affairs. So it is not surprising that it has proven difficult to gain consensus within the Security Council, let alone among the wider UN membership, both on what constitutes the new threats and how best to respond to them. There was no explicit Security Council authorization for the Kosovo and Iraq wars, and only an implied authorization for using force against Afghanistan. There has been no agreement on what to do with regard to Darfur, despite an international finding that the situation constitutes a very grave humanitarian situation and repeated, post-Rwanda exhortations that the international community must "never again" stand by as genocide unfolds. And there has been no agreement on imposing real sanctions or any other punitive action in regard to Iran's violation of the NPT, nor has there been any Security

Council response to the discovery that a Pakistani scientist (with or without official connivance) for years ran a veritable nuclear Wal-Mart, selling his knowledge and wares to anyone willing to pay.

In short, the concept of an international system composed of wholly independent, autonomous nation-states that are fundamentally equal and pose a threat only when one state attacks another no longer accords with the real world of today. Therefore, the standards for intervention, as well as the structures for making decisions on whether to intervene, must be adapted to today's realities. The notion of sovereignty as an absolute right to noninterference must be reformulated to recognize that sovereignty entails real responsibilities—both with respect to those who live within the state and with regard to internal developments that can have an impact on those who live outside it.

This changing concept of sovereignty—the notion of sovereignty as responsibility—has become increasingly accepted in recent years. The first step in this direction was the growing recognition that states have a *responsibility to protect* their own citizens from genocide, mass killing, and other gross violations of human rights.[16] The next step is to recognize that the notion extends to other areas as well. It is increasingly evident that states now also have a *responsibility to prevent* developments on their territory that pose a threat to the security of others—such as developments relating to weapons of mass destruction (such as their acquisition or the failure to secure weapons, materials, or deadly agents against possible theft or diversion); the harboring, supporting, or training of terrorists; or environmental dangers (for example, failing to prevent the spread of dangerous diseases or the destruction of rain forests).[17] Because in each of these instances what happens inside a state has consequences outside its borders, what occurs there is of importance not just to the state concerned but to everyone who is or could be affected by its actions or inactions.

The emergence of a new norm of state responsibility raises the important question of what should happen when states fail to meet their responsibilities. The world's leaders, meeting at the UN's sixtieth anniversary summit, already made clear that when a state is unable or unwilling to live up to its responsibility to protect its own people, then the responsibility for doing so falls on the international community. "We are prepared to take collective action, in a timely and decisive manner, through the Security Council . . . should peaceful means prove inadequate and national authorities manifestly fail to protect their populations."[18] Similarly, a state's failure to meet its responsibility to prevent internal developments that threaten other states implies that the responsibility to do so falls to the international community. And the most effective way for doing so will often involve preventive action. Indeed, the best time and most effective way to defeat many of the new threats is before they are imminent—*before* enough fissile material has been produced to make nuclear weapons, *before* weapons in unsecured sites or deadly diseases in laboratories have been stolen, *before* terrorists have been fully trained or are able to fully hatch their plots, *before* large-scale killing or ethnic cleansing has occurred, and *before* a deadly pathogen has mutated and spread around the globe.

Of course, in many of these cases military intervention is not the only, or even the preferred, means for dealing with an emerging threat. As James Steinberg notes in his chapter on weapons of mass destruction, there often are good alternatives.[19] Yet, to address this and other new threats, force will sometimes be necessary. When it is, it often is best used early, before threats have been fully formed, since this will likely reduce the associated costs and enhance the probability of success. The problem with the Bush doctrine, then, is not that it relies on preventive force too much but that it has conceived of its use too narrowly—primarily to deal with terrorism and as a means of forcible regime change. "The number of cases in which it might be justified will always be small," warned Rice shortly after the administration's National Security Strategy was released.[20] And because its use is reserved for truly exceptional circumstances ("The threat must be very grave. And the risks of waiting must far outweigh the risks of action," Rice cautioned), the decision to use preventive force must remain a purely national one. "While the United States will constantly strive to enlist the support of the international community, we will not hesitate to act alone, if necessary, to exercise our right of self-defense by acting preemptively."[21]

That is all well and good when the threat is clearly targeted at one's national territory or vital interests. But the insistence that states individually—or at least the United States itself—must have the right to decide when preemption is justified is clearly problematic when the threats concerned are global in scope and affect the security of many other countries. Under these circumstances, the decision to use force preemptively cannot be purely a national one. Who, then, should decide?

Who Decides?

For all its flaws, the UN Security Council remains the preferred vehicle for authorizing the use of force in cases other than self-defense, not the least because since the end of the cold war, it has been seen as the most legitimate forum for making these decisions. Consider this: before the Gulf War in 1991, the Security Council had authorized the use of force beyond traditional peacekeeping operations on only two occasions (Korea and the Congo); since then it has authorized force no less than seventeen times in places all around the world.[22] Even in the case of the Iraq war, the Bush administration, while it failed to obtain an explicit Security Council authorization, nevertheless argued that war was authorized under prior UN resolutions.[23]

Yet in practice the Security Council has not been able to agree in many instances on what internal developments would constitute a threat requiring a forceful response, and it is unlikely to do so in the future. The UN members—including the Security Council and its five permanent members—are deeply divided over the meaning of sovereignty in the contemporary world. Russia, China, and a host of developing nations continue to view absolute sovereignty as the defining principle of international affairs, and they steadfastly maintain that a country's borders demarcate an international no-go zone. What happens within the borders of a state is strictly the concern of the regime that governs that territory, not of anyone else. That is not a view acceptable to the United States and many other countries, which argue that since what happens within states can have profound consequences for others, sovereignty is not just a right but also entails responsibilities that states must fulfill if intervention in their internal affairs is to be avoided. Until the UN members, in particular all of the Security Council's permanent members, fully embrace the logic of state responsibility, investing sole decisionmaking authority with the United Nations is a recipe for indecision and inaction—and increased insecurity.

What are the alternatives? One alternative to Security Council approval is to accept the legitimacy of interventions approved by regional organizations. The model for this is Kosovo, where NATO decided to intervene to prevent a humanitarian calamity, even though the Security Council had failed to authorize the action. Regional organizations are a particularly appealing venue for deciding on the use of force since there is likely to be a great deal of convergence between those who bear the costs and those who reap the benefits of the action. Moreover, when all of the countries in the region reach a similar conclusion as to the necessity and efficacy of preventive action, the legitimacy of such action will be very much enhanced.

Of course, reliance on regional organizations is no panacea. Some threats are global rather than regional in scope and thus beyond the purview of any one regional organization to handle. There is also the danger that a regional organization may be little more than a pawn of a dominant member. One need only think of the decision of the Association of Eastern Caribbean States to endorse the 1983 intervention in Grenada, the role of Russia in the Commonwealth of Independent States, or, to a lesser extent, the role of Nigeria in the Economic Community of West African States. In addition, regional organizations may also suffer from the same problem of asymmetry as exists in the Security Council (consider the problems within the Organization for Security and Cooperation in Europe when dealing with Kosovo). And, finally, in some cases (as in much of Asia), there may be no meaningful regional organization to authorize a decision to use force.

Which leaves the alternative, should the UN or regional route fail, of relying on a coalition of like-minded states to legitimate decisionmaking on the use of force. Since democracies have a particular interest in upholding the norm of state responsibility, a coalition of democracies would provide such an alternative.[24] Democracies understand that in an era of global politics, international peace and justice rest on protecting the rights of individuals. Nation-state sovereignty can no longer be the sole organizing principle of international politics. Since what happens within a state matters to people living outside it, tackling these internal developments cooperatively is vital to the security and well-being of all. Threats to security arising within certain states are matters of concern to the commons and so must yield to legitimate cooperative action arising from the commons. Democracies are open to cooperation to preserve the common good—it is the very essence of how they govern within their own societies, after all—in a way that nondemocracies very often are not. That is why the decision of states to intervene in the affairs of another state is legitimate if it rests with the democratically chosen representatives of the people and not when it depends on the personal whims of autocrats or oligarchs.

No doubt, many will object to this alternative as drawing the decisionmaking circle too narrowly, since by any reasonable count no more than a third of current UN member countries are true democracies—meaning that such countries not only have elected governments but have had, for a sustained period of time, a constitutional system that guarantees their citizens clear political and civil rights. This being the case, a decision reached by a minority of countries can never be truly legitimate—or so many argue. But this argument equates legitimacy with universality—a common conceit of UN spokesmen and all too many of the world's countries. It reduces the concept of legitimacy to a procedural question: the number of states or votes one can marshal in support of a given action will determine that action's legitimacy. The nature of the action itself—or of the states consenting to it—matters little, if at all.

This is a deeply flawed conception of legitimacy. Surely the rightness or wrongness of a particular course of action ought at least in part to reside in the nature of the action being contemplated. Indeed, the failure to garner widespread support for forceful action when it may be necessary to reverse a terrible wrong (as, for example, in the case of genocide or widespread humanitarian atrocities) would hardly render such inaction legitimate. Similarly, it surely matters as much to the legitimacy of a given action which states support the action as how many support it. Would anyone seriously argue that an action supported by the world's many authoritarian countries would, by garnering more votes, be legitimate in a way that an action supported by the world's democracies would not? Or, conversely, would anyone seriously want to suggest that efforts to stop the slaughter in Darfur lack legitimacy because Sudan, China, Iran, Russia, and North Korea refuse to go along? If so, that is a notion of legitimacy that has lost any sense of, well, legitimacy.

Of course, as Iraq showed, a concert of democracies hardly guarantees consensus on what must be done in particular case; it just is more likely to produce legitimate consensus than in a larger and more diverse group like the UN. Moreover, the experience of organizations of democracies such as NATO and the European Union makes clear that having available a regular framework and structure for debating and reaching decisions on matters as important as the use of force is often more of a help than a hindrance. The need to debate, assess, and reassess an issue or action enhances the likelihood that the ultimate decision will be a better one than would otherwise be the case. The nations of the West relied on such debate to keep their democracies at home healthy and effective, and they relied on debate within NATO to chart a wise and effective course to fight and win the cold war over many decades. The world's democracies should continue to be relied upon to help reach wise and effective decisions on the use of force in the future.

Of course, if the United States is to commit itself to working with its democratic partners on these central issues, then the other democracies, too, have a major responsibility. They must come to the table not just prepared to debate Washington but also fully prepared to implement the decisions that are reached. This means they must both possess the capacity to deploy a significant amount of force to the most likely loci of conflict (which now spread around the globe) and be demonstrably willing to employ that force when necessary and appropriate. The essential deal to be struck between the United States and its democratic partners on the question of using force must be a true bargain—a two-way street. While Washington must commit to involving the other democracies in decisions on using force in cases other than self-defense, its democratic partners must commit to bringing real capabilities to the table and to using them when a decision to do so is reached.

Conclusion

This is an era in which the use of military force remains a central preoccupation of states and their leaders. In many respects the demand for forceful intervention is likely to continue to grow, as it has ever since the cold war ended. Distance no longer wards off dangers far away; the global interconnectedness of these times means that developments anywhere can have major consequences for people everywhere. An effective security policy must determine ways to intervene early enough to ensure that small, manageable threats do not become big, unmanageable ones. In most instances such intervention can be cooperative, emphasizing diplomacy and economic assistance. But some situations will require the threat or use of military force—and when they do, the use of force early is likely to be more effective and less costly than waiting until it is a last resort.

Preemption, in other words, is here to stay. The hope for the future is that when it comes to making decisions on whether or not to intervene preemptively, the process of deciding will involve detailed information, probing analysis, in-depth discussion and debate, and a constant willingness to reassess the evidence. It also requires a genuine willingness to bring others into the deliberations—in particular America's democratic allies, whose perspective on these issues matters greatly. When it comes to the use of force, the American and global debate often narrows the choice to doing it within the framework of the United Nations or going it alone. This is a false choice. An effective and viable alternative to multilateral paralysis and unilateral action is for the United States to work with its democratic partners around the world to meet and defeat the global threats of our age.

Notes

This chapter draws on a number of previous writings that stem in part from the Brookings Institution Project on Force and Legitimacy in a Changing World, including Ivo Daalder and James Steinberg, "The Future of Preemption," *American Interest* 1 (Winter 2005): 30–39; Ivo Daalder and James Lindsay, "Democracies of the World, Unite," *American Interest* 2 (January-February 2007): 5–15; and Ivo Daalder and Robert Kagan, "The Use of Force," in *Bridging the Foreign Policy Divide*, edited by Tod Lindberg, Derek Chollet, and David Shorr (Muscatine, Iowa: Stanley Foundation, forthcoming).

1. George W. Bush, "State of the Union Address," January 29, 2002 (www.whitehouse.gov/news/releases/2002/01/20020129-11.html).

2. George W. Bush, "Remarks by the President at 2002 Graduation Exercise of the United States Military Academy," June 1, 2002 (www.whitehouse.gov/news/releases/2002/06/20020601-3.html).

3. Wolf Blitzer, "Search for the 'Smoking Gun,'" CNN, January 10, 2003 (www.cnn.com/2003/US/01/10/wbr.smoking.gun).

4. White House, *The National Security Strategy of the United States of America* (September 2002), p. 15 (www.whitehouse.gov/nsc/nss.pdf).

5. "Prime Minister Warns of Continuing Global Terror Threat," March 5, 2004 (www.number-10.gov.uk/output/Page5461.asp).

6. French Ministry of Defense, "2003–2008 Military Programme, Bill of Law," September 11, 2002 (www.info-france-usa.org/atoz/mindefa.pdf), p. 6.

7. Quoted in Sophie Lambroschini, "Russia: Moscow Struggles to Clarify Stance on Preemptive Force," Radio Free Europe–Radio Liberty, October 14, 2003 (www.globalsecurity.org/military/library/news/2003/10/mil-031014-rferl-171155.htm).

8. Sergei Ivanov, "Russia Must Be Strong," *Wall Street Journal*, January 11, 2006 (online.wsj.com/article/SB113695268001343534.html?mod=opinion_main_commentaries).

9. Quoted in Martin Fackler, "Japan Finds Still Sterner Words for North Korea's Missile Test," *New York Times,* July 11, 2006 (www.nytimes.com/2006/07/11/world/asia/11missiles.html).

10. Kofi Annan, "Address to the General Assembly," September 23, 2003 (www.un.org/webcast/ga/58/statements/sg2eng030923).

11. High-Level Panel on Threats, Challenges and Change, *A More Secure World: Our Shared Responsibility,* December 2004 (www.un.org/secureworld/report3.pdf), pp. 63–64.

12. United Nations, *In Larger Freedom: Towards Development, Security and Human Rights for All,* Report of the Secretary General, March 2005 (www.un.org/largerfreedom/contents.htm).

13. High-Level Panel, *A More Secure World,* p. 64.

14. Ivo Daalder and James Steinberg, "New Rules on When to Use Force," *Financial Times,* August 2, 2004.

15. White House, *National Security Strategy,* p. 4.

16. International Commission on Intervention and State Sovereignty, *The Responsibility to Protect,* September 2001 (www.iciss.ca/pdf/Commission-Report.pdf).

17. For a similar argument, confined to weapons of mass destruction, see Lee Feinstein and Anne-Marie Slaughter, "A Duty to Prevent," *Foreign Affairs* 83 (January-February 2004): 136–50.

18. UN General Assembly, "2005 World Summit Outcome," A/60/L.1 (New York: September 15, 2005), p. 31.

19. See Steinberg, chapter 2, in this volume.

20. Condoleezza Rice, "A Balance of Power That Favors Freedom," address to the Manhattan Institute, October 1, 2002 (www.manhattan-institute.org/html/wl2002.htm).

21. White House, *National Security Strategy,* p. 6.

22. Eric Voeten, "The Political Origins of the UN Security Council's Ability to Legitimize the Use of Force," *International Organizations* 59 (Summer 2005): 531.

23. Notably, resolution 678, which authorized the Gulf War; 687, which established conditions for a cease-fire of that war; and 1441, which provided Baghdad with one final chance to implement prior resolutions. See John D. Negroponte, "Letter to the President of the Security Council," March 20, 2003 (www.un.int/usa/s2003_351.pdf).

24. The case for creating a "concert of democracies," is detailed in Ivo Daalder and James Lindsay, "Democracies of the World, Unite," *American Interest* 2, no. 3 (2007): 5–15. For variants on this alternative, see also Stanley Hoffmann, *World Disorders: Troubled Peace in the Post–Cold War Era* (Lanham, Md.: Rowman and Littlefield, 1998), p. 80; Thomas M. Nichols, "Anarchy and Order in the New Age of Prevention," *World Policy Journal* 22 (Fall 2005): 14–20; and G. John Ikenberry and Anne-Marie Slaughter, *Forging a World under Law and Liberty: U.S. National Security in the 21st Century,* September 2006 (www.wws.princeton.edu/ppns/report/FinalReport.pdf), pp. 25–26, 61.

CHAPTER TWO

Weapons of Mass Destruction
and the Use of Force

JAMES B. STEINBERG

THE BUSH ADMINISTRATION's National Security Strategy Report of 2002 touched off a vigorous debate in the United States and abroad over whether and when it is appropriate to use force other than in response to an attack (imminent or actual). In the report, the administration stated:

> The United States has long maintained the option of preemptive actions to counter a sufficient threat to our national security. The greater the threat, the greater is the risk of inaction—and the more compelling the case for taking anticipatory action to defend ourselves, even if uncertainty remains as to the time and place of the enemy's attack. To forestall or prevent such hostile acts by our adversaries, the United States will, if necessary, act preemptively.[1]

While many of the administration's critics denounced this new and dangerous policy, the administration touted the need to go beyond past practice, stating that it was warranted by the novel and dangerous threats facing the United States.[2] But the use of preventive force—and the debates over its legality and wisdom—predates the Bush administration's post–September 11 strategy.

Given the centrality of this issue in contemporary international affairs, it is vitally important to understand whether it is possible to achieve a new consensus on the preventive use of force that is both principled and can achieve broad agreement in the United States and the wider international community.[3] The first part of this paper therefore examines the arguments for and against modifying the traditional doctrine on the use of force and presents a set of criteria for using preventive force in dealing with proliferation of weapons of mass destruction. The latter part draws on a series of conferences with international policymakers and analysts around the world, organized by the Brookings Institution, to assess the degree to which this new approach can achieve widespread international acceptability.

Traditional Doctrine Limiting Use of Force in International Relations

The debate over when and under what circumstances the United States should use force preventively has taken on a new intensity with the end of the cold war and, in particular, after the terrorist attacks of September 11, 2001. Throughout U.S. history, American leaders have ritually repeated as declaratory policy that the United States should not and would not use force except in response to an armed attack or the threat of imminent attack against the United States or its citizens, although the actual U.S. experience has been more complex.[4] As the United States became part of formal alliances and took on collective security responsibilities after World War II, these criteria were expanded to include attacks on others to whom the United States had treaty obligations (for example, article 5 of the North Atlantic Treaty that established NATO, and bilateral security agreements with Japan, Korea, Thailand) or as part of a signatory's responsibilities under Chapter 7 of the UN Charter.

The formal rule is enshrined in the UN Charter itself, which prohibits the use of force in international relations (Article 2[4]) with two exceptions: it is permitted either pursuant to a decision by the UN Security Council acting under Chapter 7 in response to threats to international peace and security, or under Article 51 for self-defense.[5] The rationale for these limitations is deeply rooted in the conviction that arose out of the experience of two world wars: that aggression poses the principal threat to peace and security. As a result, international law has sought to delegitimize the use of force by an individual state acting on its own, except to defend against aggression. Implicit in this view is a belief that internal arrangements within a state, however repugnant, posed little threat to the security or well-being of others as long as that state did not forcibly venture beyond its borders. Legitimacy was defined primarily in this status quo–preserving sense: it was legitimate to resist the encroachment of others but not to encroach on others, irrespective of the reason for encroachment.

Chapter 7 of the UN Charter expanded the permissible justification for using force but sought to hedge against the danger of a too-easy resort to force by establishing a high procedural hurdle—approval by the Security Council. Legitimacy in this case springs more from the legitimacy of the "deciders" than from the substantive justification for using force.

The idealized model of the UN Charter never fully corresponded to how policymakers thought about the international system; for most of its history, the United States did "care" about the internal affairs of other nations it considered important, either because of their geographic proximity (as in the case of U.S. attitudes toward governments in the Western Hemisphere) or because of their real or perceived strategic significance. But most of the time, U.S. policymakers sought to couch these interventions in the agreed doctrinal framework (or conducted them through covert or indirect means), even if it seemed to stretch the plain meaning of the words beyond recognition.

Changing International Environment in the Post–Cold War, Post–September 11 World

By the 1990s, the basic disconnect between international reality and the principle of nonintervention became clear enough to force a reexamination of the traditional declaratory doctrine. The impetus came from two distinct directions: a growing uneasiness with a principle of international law that appeared to require states to acquiesce in gross violations of human rights, and a recognition that a nation might act in ways that posed unacceptable security risks to others, even in the absence of an overt use of force against its neighbors. The experiences in the Balkans and Rwanda provided the context for the first critique of the traditional rules; the growing concern about nuclear proliferation and states that harbor or support terrorism, particularly after September 11, underpinned the second critique.

The violent ethnic conflict that followed the breakup of Yugoslavia highlighted two interrelated challenges concerning the use of force in post–cold war conflict: what are legitimate grounds for using force, and who has the right to decide to use force?

The terrorist attacks of 2001 also led to a debate over the continued validity of the traditional rules on the use of force (regarding both when and who decides). President Bush argued, in a series of speeches and later in his first National Security Strategy Report, that in a world characterized by "rogue" states and terrorist groups prepared to use weapons of mass destruction, the United States must be willing to use force preventively, acting alone if necessary, to guarantee its security.

The debate has often been divided into questions of legitimacy and those of effectiveness, although in practice the two are so deeply intertwined as to be practically indistinguishable.[6] And now that the bright lines governing the legitimate use of force have become blurred by the changed international environment and emerging humanitarian norms, there is a need for greater clarity about what considerations should govern the use of force. Broadly speaking, these considerations can be divided into four questions:

—When should force be used?
—What kind of force should be used?
—What are the alternatives to the use of force?
—Who should decide on the use of force?

WHEN SHOULD FORCE BE USED?

The contemporary debate now centers primarily on four kinds of circumstances (beyond aggression) that might justify the resort to force: military operations against terrorists; stopping the spread of weapons of mass destruction (WMD); humanitarian crises; and interventions in the case of state failure. This chapter focuses on the second of these circumstances, the use of force for counterproliferation purposes aimed at eliminating dangerous capabilities related to mass destruction.

There are a number of powerful arguments in favor of using force preventively in the case of nascent WMD capabilities. First, and most compelling, is that in some cases the mere possession of such a dangerous capability may be judged unacceptable, either because it frees the possessing state to act more dangerously toward its people or others, believing that the possession of WMD insulates it against attack, or because it might encourage others to seek similar capabilities, leading to further destabilizing proliferation. In these cases, whether the possessor intends to use the WMD is unrelated to the danger to international peace and security, so the traditional test of "imminent threat of attack" is irrelevant. Second, the threat of the use of force may help to deter a potential acquirer from pursing the dangerous capability in the first place, or lead it to the negotiating table, as was arguably the case with North Korea in 1994. Third, some aspects of imminent danger may be hard to detect, such as the transfer of WMD from a state to a terrorist organization; so in the case of states with ties to terrorists, possession may be the closest one can get to a warning. Fourth, even if there is a "warning," it may be too late to do anything about it—as, for example, with a ballistic missile attack where, either because of short flight times or inadequate defense capabilities, the attack cannot be stopped.

More generally, using force preventively against WMD capabilities has strong appeal because of the potentially devastating consequences of either failure of warning or inadequacy of defense. Few leaders would want to contemplate the consequences of a successful nuclear or biological attack on a major population center.

Not surprisingly, then, in actual practice, preventive force has either been used or considered under a number of circumstances since the dawn of the nuclear era. The desirability and feasibility of preventive strikes figured prominently in the debate about U.S. and Soviet nuclear doctrine and played a major role in shaping force structure (for example, counterforce capability, the evolution of the triad, and survivability of command and control). Although preventive force was in fact never employed, it was seriously debated both in connection with the Cuban missile crisis and the nascent Chinese nuclear capability in the 1960s.

More recently, preventive force has been used to thwart the development of WMD capabilities—by Israel in its 1981 attack on Iraq's Osirak reactor; in August 1998 by the Clinton administration against what it believed to be a chemical weapons facility in Sudan; and later that same year against Iraqi WMD-related sites after the expulsion of UN arms inspectors (Operation Desert Fox). The most prominent recent case, of course, was the Bush administration's intervention in Iraq, where the latent threat of Iraq's WMD programs was a major justification for the action. To the list should be added Secretary of Defense William Perry's threat to use force against the North Korean reactor at Yongbyon in 1994 (which was obviated by the North Koreans' decision to suspend pluto-nium reprocessing under the Agreed Framework). The possibility of pre-ventive interdiction also lies at the heart of the Bush administration's Pro-liferation Security Initiative, an approach that was prefigured by the Clinton administration's efforts to stop a perceived transfer of WMD capability from China to Iran on the ship *Yin He* in 1993.

Despite the evident appeal of the use of preventive force in this context, there are also important reasons for caution. First, using force may not be the only way to stop proliferation; over the past decades, a number of states have voluntarily given up WMD capabilities (South Africa, Ukraine, Belarus, and Kazakhstan) or their nascent nuclear programs (Argentina and Brazil). Second, the use or threat of force against WMD capabilities could have the unintended consequence of persuading others that they should *speed up* their efforts to acquire such capabilities to gain a measure of protection against attack or lead them to conceal dangerous facilities. Third, these attacks could be of limited effectiveness if facilities are hidden or dispersed, or if the country has the ability to rapidly recon-stitute them. Fourth, even if effective, such attacks could have severe col-lateral consequences through, for example, the release of deadly chemi-cals, radioactive material, or pathogens. Fifth, the use of force under these circumstances could provoke retaliation, which could worsen security. Sixth, attacking facilities of a rogue regime could have the unintended consequence of rallying support for a dangerous government that might otherwise be unpopular with its own citizens, thus strengthening its hold on power. If the intelligence is considered flawed or the action widely considered illegitimate, the attack could also lead to support—though probably just rhetorical—for the regime from other countries, which might not have otherwise been forthcoming. Seventh, there are also prob-lems of consistency since in some cases the acquisition of WMD has not triggered the preventive use of force—for example, in the cases of India and Pakistan. Eighth, as the Iraq case so vividly illustrates (as well as the controversy over the suspected North Korean facility at Kumchang-ri in 1998–99, and the ex post facto debate over the bombing of the al-Shifa plant in Sudan), there is the danger that the intelligence providing the rationale for an attack will be challenged, with all of the adverse conse-quences that has been shown to bring. Even if the preattack intelligence appears to be sound, postattack questions can undermine the credibility and legitimacy of the decision to use force.

The role of prevention remains a hot topic today, given the considerable discussion about the desirability and potential efficacy of military strikes against Iran's developing nuclear capability as well as the debate both in the United States and Japan over a possible preventive strike against North Korea's ballistic missile launch capability. All the considerations outlined above come into play in the current crisis with Iran. There are powerful reasons to fear the consequences of an Iranian nuclear weapons capability, including the effect on regional stability, the danger that it will promote further nuclear proliferation, and the risk that the weapons or weapons-grade material might fall (intentionally or unintentionally) into the hands of terrorist groups. Yet all of the dangers of preventive action identified above could be realized if the United States (or others) decides to use preventive force against the Iranian enrichment program.

WHAT KIND OF FORCE SHOULD BE APPLIED?

Once the case has been made for using force, the question that then arises is what kind of force should be applied. Broadly speaking, this can be divided into two categories: targeted use of force against particular dangerous individuals or capabilities, or "total war–regime change"— although in practice there is something of a continuum.

At first blush, it would seem easier to justify the targeted use of force. Killing known or suspected terrorists, or destroying or interdicting WMD capabilities, seems to fit the traditional just war considerations of proportionality and limiting collateral harm.

Yet there are circumstances where a more far-ranging use of force— regime change—may be justified, largely on the grounds of necessity. With respect to WMD, the ability of a regime to conceal capabilities, or to reconstitute them quickly after a more limited attack, could provide a rationale for using force to eliminate the regime. This was a consideration in the case of Iraq (in light of its repeated failures to comply with UN resolutions on disarmament), and for some this is the only solution for Iran and North Korea. In the case of terrorists acquiring WMD, the demonstrated willingness of a state to harbor dangerous individuals and groups could provide an acceptable justification, as near-universal support for the invasion of Afghanistan demonstrates. In the case of state failure, there may be a need to impose control amounting to trusteeship.

There are obviously strong prudential arguments against the use of force to effect regime change. First, with respect to most threats emanating from states, including so-called rogues, there is reason to believe, notwithstanding the assertions of the Bush administration's first National Security Strategy Report in 2002, that deterrence or containment can be effective; most rogue leaders relish their hold on power. Second, there are substantial differences among rogue states that make it hard to generalize about which rogue regimes are too dangerous to be allowed to continue; at various times the rogue list has included Cuba, yet few seriously contemplate (at least since the 1961 Bay of Pigs invasion) forceful regime change there. The use of force to change governments could have the effect of creating a much more violent international environment, eroding the constraints against aggression. Perhaps most important, the high costs in blood and treasure of a military intervention to bring about regime change and the uncertain outcome make it difficult to arrive at a convincing judgment that the attacker will necessarily be better off after a regime change. In the case of WMD possession, there is no guarantee that the successor regime will not pursue such capabilities, and, in any event, as Iraq shows, the fallout within the attacked country and the region can be substantial. Moreover, the use of force to change a regime without Security Council approval can come at a high cost to the attacker's prestige and "soft power," possibly generating a negative long-term cost-benefit outcome even if the operation is reasonably successful in narrow terms. Thus there is good reason to conclude that the use of force to bring about regime change is highly problematic and should be reserved for cases of grave risk where all other measures have clearly been exhausted, and should almost never be undertaken unilaterally.[7]

Irrespective of whether the proposed use of force is limited or "total," there is a question of whether the use of force should be overt or covert.[8] Because of the norms against using force preventively and the possible adverse consequences, it will be tempting in many cases to resort to covert tools, particularly where the goal is to eliminate terrorists or dangerous capabilities. The covert use of force helps minimize the precedent-setting effect of the action compared with an acknowledged use of force, and it may make it possible for the target to avoid being drawn into a series of escalatory responses that neither side desires. Nonetheless, there are many familiar drawbacks to covert action beyond those associated with unwanted disclosure. In planning any covert action, the restricted circle involved in the decisionmaking may exclude important information or full consideration of the issues. It may also make the covert action more likely out of a belief that adverse consequences can be avoided. Because such action is likely to be unilateral and certainly without institutional endorsement or visible allies, it has the problems of legitimacy discussed below (see "Who Should Decide?"). Thus the basic considerations that lead to a highly restrictive set of rules governing unilateral preventive action apply with even greater force to unilateral covert action.

ARE THERE ALTERNATIVES?

In judging the legitimacy and appropriateness of the preventive use of force, it is important to consider the question, "as opposed to what?" Although there are substantial costs and risks to acting preventively, the calculation may still be favorable in light of the alternatives.

Irrespective of which kind of force is chosen, there is a widely shared understanding that the decision should be based on a convincing conclusion that alternatives other than force would not be effective in achieving the stated goal. Virtually no one argues that force is just one of many tools in the policy kit; from both a moral and practical standpoint, there is a strong presumption that the use of force should be a last resort.

To some degree there has been a tendency in recent years to downplay the potential effectiveness of alternatives to the use of force. In particular, questions about the effectiveness of sanctions and their collateral humanitarian costs have complicated the question of how hard and fast the last-resort rule should be.

The general preference to regard force as a last resort clearly does not mean that in all cases all other alternatives must actually have been tried and failed. In some cases, it may be apparent that nothing else would work, and, in other cases, the speed with which a danger is unfolding and the risk of a fait accompli may make formal exhaustion of alternatives impractical. But there is a danger that alternatives—such as containment, sanctions, or diplomacy—will be too easily discarded based on previous failures of these policy tools or a particular administration's attitude about their effectiveness more generally. Given the costs associated with the decision to use force, there should be a high burden on those proposing to use force to show that other alternatives have been tried and failed or that they would necessarily prove ineffective or counterproductive.

Unlike the scenario of using preventive force against committed terrorists, there do appear to be viable alternatives, in some cases, for dealing with rogue regimes. There is reason to believe that deterrence continues to have value against most states, however "roguish," in particular with regard to their use of WMD. Deterrence may also be useful for dissuading rogue states from transferring WMD to terrorists: although such transfers might take place clandestinely, the risk that the transfer will either be detected as it occurs or attributed after the fact, leading to the use of force against the provider, could outweigh the benefits of the transfer, particularly since any regime that might be tempted to transfer these capabilities also would worry that the WMD might be used against it. This deterrent effect can be enhanced by improving the technology of attribution (the ability to trace the source, for example, of fissile material or pathogens) or by announcing in advance that a particular state will be held responsible for the acts of a particular group of terrorists, even in the absence of specific evidence of transfer (so-called deemed attribution). Of course, in the latter case there is a risk that an unsuspected group or individual will commit an act with the expectation or hope that responsibility will be deemed to the "usual suspect(s)."

There has been considerable discussion about "smart" sanctions (such as targeting the assets and travels of leaders, or criminal indictments) as an alternative both to force and broad economic sanctions. Although these can clearly be positive additions to the policy toolkit, it is questionable how effective these will be in dealing with regimes and leaders that are already deeply isolated (such as in North Korea).

Deterrence is more problematic as a tool against acquisition of WMD. Given the track record to date (the international community's acquiescence in the case of the Indian, Pakistani, and now North Korean nuclear programs, compounded by the international backlash against the intervention in Iraq), it would be reasonable for a would-be acquirer to assume that there is little likelihood that force would be used to forestall or eliminate its acquisition of WMD capabilities. Moreover, the sanctions fatigue and collateral humanitarian costs associated with sanctions in Iraq suggest that coercive measures short of force may not be very effective.

However, the successes in achieving denuclearization without force (most notably in South Africa but also Ukraine, Belarus, and Kazakhstan, as well as the protonuclear programs in Argentina and Brazil) suggest that, at least over time, there is an alternative, namely, containment—in effect, waiting either for regime change (South Africa, Brazil, Argentina) or for circumstances to change the acquirer's cost-benefit calculations. Waiting can be coupled with other measures that affect cost-benefit calculations, such as sanctions (the sanctions against South Africa were not imposed because of its nuclear program but were directed at the regime and therefore had a similar effect). Containment can also be buttressed by providing security guarantees to neighboring countries, thus lessening the blackmail effect and therefore the adverse costs of acquiescence. Here the credibility of the security guarantees will be crucial.

"Denial" strategies (preventing bad actors from acquiring dangerous capabilities) are also an important alternative. The case for this approach is particularly compelling in the nuclear context, where the need to acquire fissile material and the technology to produce it is still a major barrier to acquiring a nuclear capability. In the biological and chemical context, denial strategies are increasingly futile, as the know-how and materials have become so widespread that supplier regimes and control of materials are not likely to be of much use, other than providing a normative framework for justifying the use of force (for example, against a country that is developing clandestine programs in violation of international treaties like the Chemical Weapons Convention, whether or not the country is a signatory to the agreement).

Denial strategies include supplier regimes, like the Wassenaar Arrangement, the Nuclear Suppliers Group, and the Australia Group, which seek to control the export of advanced conventional, nuclear, chemical, and biological technologies, as well as interdiction strategies, like the Proliferation Security Initiative. Interdiction should be considered a preventive use of force, in the same way as the Israeli attack on Osirak or Operation Desert Fox. But, to the extent that the use of force happens in transit, particularly international waters, the costs and risks associated may be less than an attack within the "country of concern." But even if the interdiction is during transit, there remain some risks, as the U.S. interdiction of the Chinese ship *Yin He,* mistakenly suspected of carrying chemical weapon components to Iran, illustrates.

The final alternative is conditional engagement, used to good effect to bring an end to the Libyan nuclear program and, to a lesser extent, in connection with the Agreed Framework governing North Korea's nuclear program.[9] In the case of Libya, the key elements were a combination of pressure (sanctions) and incentives (normalization). In the case of North Korea, the threat of force was more explicit, ranging from the warnings by Secretary Perry to the preliminary force deployments that gave credibility to the threat.[10] The benefits of this approach are apparent. The costs of it include legitimating bad regimes (in most cases, regimes that seek to acquire WMD also oppress their own people and are often involved with terrorists, international criminals, and drug dealers) and providing incentives for bad behavior (both for the country in question, as in the case of North Korea, and for others who might seek to emulate the strategy).

WHO SHOULD DECIDE?

The preceding discussion shows that the contemporary international environment requires a rethinking of criteria for when to use force, beyond the narrow circumstances currently endorsed by conventional international law. But if each country is free to decide for itself when these expanded criteria are met, there is a serious danger that the bar to using force will be lowered dramatically, increasing the risk of international anarchy. The question, then, is how to respond to the emerging threats while minimizing the perils associated with more expansive criteria for the use of force.

The underlying premise of the UN Charter was that, except in the relatively narrow case of self-defense against aggression, the decision to use force should be reserved exclusively for the Security Council. The UN secretary general's High-Level Panel on Threats, Challenges and Change acknowledged that the world had changed since the end of World War II, justifying the use of force in a broader category of circumstances, but it largely accepted that the only acceptable way to confront these new dangers was under the aegis of the Security Council.

There are very good reasons why Security Council approval is highly desirable in almost any case where force is contemplated. Where the exercise of force is seen to be legitimate, it is easier to gain support for the military action itself, thus lessening the financial and human costs, reducing the risk that others will try to retaliate or otherwise impose costs on the user of force, and reducing the likelihood that application of force will have the unintended effect of strengthening the very regime it was meant to constrain. It is not surprising therefore that even the Bush administration was driven to seek Security Council approval (the "second resolution") for its intervention in Iraq.

Although expanding the scope of Security Council action is certainly a valuable step, recent history powerfully suggests that this will not obviate the use of force when the council fails to act. This is due in large part to the inherent asymmetries between the costs and benefits experienced by different countries in the face of these threats. The United States, with global responsibilities and interests, perceives a broader range of threats to its security than do many other countries and may feel the need to take action even in circumstances where there is no direct danger to the United States. This was clearly the case in the Balkans, for example, in the 1990s and with respect to Iraq in 2002–03. Conversely, other members of the Security Council may believe that endorsing action under these circumstances could establish a precedent that could be used against them or their interests—again, the view of Russia and China during the Balkan conflicts—or that the collateral costs of using force for them are greater than the benefits—the view, for example, of France concerning Iraq in 2003.

There are other reasons to question the appropriateness of allowing the Security Council to be the final arbiter of the decision to use force. Although the UN carries the aura of legitimacy associated with the circumstances of its founding and the lofty principles of its charter, the reality is more complicated. It seems reasonable to question why an authoritarian government in Beijing, which seeks to insulate itself against intervention by outsiders in its internal affairs, should be allowed to block a humanitarian intervention in the Balkans. Similarly, should the Russian government, with its long history of cozy financial dealings with Iraq, be allowed to shield a regime that was believed by most to be actively pursuing dangerous WMD programs?

Thus, in some sense, the Security Council's failure to act did not per se mean that the use of force was unjustified. It has led to a search for alternatives to council authorization that preserve some of the "legitimacy" benefits of collective action, focusing on the role of regional (for example, NATO or the African Union) or other multilateral organizations. This approach has the virtue of avoiding the potential arbitrariness and other dangers of unilateral or ad hoc coalition action while avoiding likely stalemates in the Security Council. The model for this kind of approach is NATO's action in Kosovo, initiated without explicit authorization by the council.

An alternative to regional groupings is the use of "like-minded" group-ings to legitimate decisionmaking on the use of force. For example, some have suggested that a "concert of democracies" might be an appropriate forum for deciding on the use of force.[11] There are two principal argu-ments in support of this approach. First is the idea that the legitimacy of the action stems from the greater legitimacy of each of the individual gov-ernments making the decision. This would seem true to a point, but as the debates over who belongs to the community of democracies indicate, there is no bright line between states that are democratically legitimate and those that are not. The second argument is prudential: because democracies are more accountable to their people, who bear the cost of military action in blood and treasure, they are therefore less likely to use force arbitrarily. This is to a considerable extent an empirical judgment. It could be argued that recent U.S. policy, which advocates an expansive use of force, is inconsistent with this view, but the proposition can only be tested over the long term.

Further along the spectrum are ad hoc coalitions. Indisputably, the fact that more than one country has agreed on the necessity of using force adds some legitimacy in comparison with the decision of an individual nation, but the effect is limited when the mission defines the coalition rather than vice versa. Whether there is significant additional legitimacy from a "coalition of the willing" depends in part on who the members are. If the followers are heavily dependent on the lead country, such as the United States, there will be questions about whether the agreement on the necessity to act is coerced.

At the far end of the spectrum is unilateral action. The Bush adminis-tration's 2002 National Security Strategy caused great controversy in part because it seemed to elevate the legitimacy of unilateral action far beyond what is likely to prove necessary, since in almost every instance the United States is likely to get at least some backing from others. The point of this rather extreme articulation appeared to be an effort to establish that the only constraint on the use of force by the United States was domestic law. And even there, the administration has stoked controversy through a very far-reaching interpretation of the president's authority to act, even with-out the agreement of Congress, in furtherance of his responsibilities as commander in chief.[12]

Where a proposed use of force fails to gain broad-based backing (through the UN Security Council, regional organizations, and the like), the legitimacy of the action can be buttressed by linking it to broadly agreed-upon norms. Thus the United States pointed to Iraq's repeated violations of Security Council resolutions as a justification for using force and treated the lack of council action as an institutional failure rather than a reason to question the legitimacy of the coalition's action. Similar arguments could be made in connection with the potential use of force against countries such as North Korea or Iran that are building nuclear weapons capabilities in violation of their Non-Proliferation Treaty (NPT) obligations, whether or not the Security Council acts.[13]

One way to enhance the legitimacy of such norm-based action has been suggested by Robert Keohane, who proposed a formal mechanism for post hoc accountability to the international community by states that decide to use force unilaterally.[14] A state using force would have to report to the Security Council after the fact and demonstrate that its use of force conformed to the stated facts on the ground. Although the basic strategy is appealing, there is an inherent problem: this approach will tend to reward success rather than legitimate justification; when things go well, it may appear that the end justified the means whereas the fact that things go badly may not by itself mean that the decision was not reasonable at the time it was made. There are certain analogies here to both the benefits and costs of a "strict liability" approach to accountability in domestic legal systems.

International Attitudes toward Prevention and WMD

The practical and intellectual debates about the preventive use of force, especially in the case of halting the spread of WMD, are not confined to the United States. Dialogues with a number of international partners made evident the terms of the debate internationally, as well as where various countries and regions stand on the issue. The dialogues all took place in the shadow of real-world diplomacy over the Iranian nuclear program, which formed an explicit subject of conversation in all of the meetings. To a considerable degree, the discussion focused less on the legitimacy of using force preventively against actual or potential WMD targets per se and more on the efficacy of any proposed course of action.

With Iran in mind, for example, European participants in the first Brookings-sponsored U.S.-European dialogue noted that it was much easier to think about military preventive attack against a single target

(Osirak) than against a large, dispersed, and possibly concealed program, such as that of Iran. The practical considerations got a more explicit airing during the second conference with European counterparts, where both sides worked through a structured scenario designed to test the willingness to use force at various stages during the development of the Iranian nuclear program. Although both Americans and Europeans agreed that the dangers associated with an Iranian nuclear capability were "unacceptable," the European participants were much more skeptical about the desirability of acting forcefully to prevent that unacceptable outcome from materializing. Although both sides supported forceful measures to interdict WMD material in transit, the European participants balked at the use of force against targets on Iranian soil (such as surgical strikes on enrichment facilities).

The European and American discussants tended to look at the problem through different lenses. The Americans were more focused on the specific danger posed by a nuclear-armed Iran whereas the Europeans emphasized the importance of supporting the NPT. The more specific focus of the American participants buttressed a greater willingness to act while the more generalized concern of the Europeans underpinned the many practical objections to using force under these circumstances. Because the Europeans were focused on norm reinforcement, the issue of institutional legitimacy, especially Security Council approval, figured more prominently—not so much as a matter of theology but rather out of concern that the use of force to strengthen the nonproliferation norm would be undercut by an exercise that was not blessed by the council.

Somewhat surprisingly, Chinese participants also seemed prepared to accept, in principle, the possible use of preventive force to halt acquisition of WMD capability. Like the U.S. participants in the Sino-U.S. dialogue, the Chinese tended to see this in terms of specific threats—with the obvious case being the possibility that Taiwan (and perhaps Japan) would acquire nuclear weapons. (At the same time, the Chinese participants, consistent with the apparent views of the Chinese government, were much more reserved about the North Korean case, perceiving that North Korea was unlikely to use its WMD program against others or as a shield to pursue more aggressive policies.) For this reason, the Chinese, like the Americans, placed less emphasis on the need for formal international approval of action in the case of a serious threat. Some of the Chinese participants seemed willing to support an expanded view of Article 51 so as to eliminate the need for UN approval under these circumstances.

This was also the general perspective of Russian participants (at least in this group, which believed that its views reflected broader attitudes in the Russian government), who had become disenchanted with Iran and more concerned about the danger that an Iranian nuclear program might be a conduit to transferring WMD to Islamic radicals. (The Russians also held a similar concern about the Pakistani nuclear program.) Like the Chinese participants, the Russians were also more open to the expanded interpretation of Article 51 as an approach to this problem.

Based on the strong African commitment to keeping their continent a nuclear-weapons-free zone, African participants also took a fairly strong view of the desirability of enforcing the NPT, even through the use of force. While there was broad consensus on the principle that force could be an appropriate tool to halt WMD proliferation, and even though most agreed that, for example, in the case of Iran, there was a clear basis (illegal nuclear weapons program) for action, African participants focused on the difficulties and limitations of the use of force in practice.

Unsurprisingly, South Asian participants leaned more toward the European view, focusing on the universality of the norm and the legitimacy behind the action rather than on the specific danger. Since both India and Pakistan are outside the NPT, and because they consider the nuclear powers in default of their obligations under Article VI of the NPT, they questioned the legitimacy of using force to uphold its provisions. Although both Indians and Pakistanis agreed that states should be held accountable, including through the use of force in the case of transfers of WMD to terrorists (and pointed to the institutional legitimation of this principle in UN Security Council Resolution 1540), they were much more reluctant to consider the use of force in the case of state-to-state transfers, even in the case of transfers to state sponsors of terrorism.

The conversation with Mexican counterparts provided the most dramatic divergence since many of the Mexican participants took a much less alarmist view of Iran developing a nuclear capability (and indeed, more generally, of the dangers of proliferation) than participants from any other country or region in the meetings. For this reason, there was little support for using force preventively in these circumstances, even with broad international endorsement. Mexican participants were more inclined to look at the underlying reasons why states sought to acquire WMD and the responsibility that others (especially the United States) held for creating an environment where acquisition of WMD might be seen as an understandable national security strategy.

The Way Forward

There is clearly no universal consensus on the preventive use of force to halt the proliferation of WMD. But several elements stand out from our discussions.

First, *greater consistency and clarity in establishing the norms of what is and is not acceptable will strengthen support for action,* whether or not the action itself is ultimately endorsed by the Security Council. Although some countries and regions (the United States, Russia, and, surprisingly, China) placed less emphasis on universality than others (South Asia, Europe, and Mexico), there is little doubt that all would find the case for action strengthened by rules that are universal and evenly applied. In the WMD context, this means strongly considering updating the NPT to address the newly perceived dangers of the nuclear fuel cycle, building on UN Security Council Resolution 1540 to create universal obligations with respect to securing and nontransference of nuclear materials. It will also entail provision of a broader legal basis for the Proliferation Security Initiative through a treaty (perhaps under UN sponsorship). Although most of the discussions focused on the nuclear arena, similar considerations apply particularly with respect to biological weapons and the Biological Weapons Convention.

Second, *stronger agreed factual predicates will help generate support for action and strengthen legitimacy.* For many participants the undercurrent of anxiety about the preventive use of force and WMD was attributable to the debacle over the Iraq intelligence (and the controversy over al-Shifa before it). Strong, ideally international, fact finding could help address the problem by strengthening both the authority and capabilities (especially of inspection and analysis) of organizations such as the International Atomic Energy Agency and the Organization for the Prohibition of Chemical Weapons. The vacuum associated with the failure to negotiate transparency and verification measures for the Biological and Toxin Weapons Convention needs to be filled, and the enforcement protocols must be strengthened.

Third, *the Security Council members need to commit to stronger action short of force when treaty commitments regarding WMD are violated.* The persistent flouting of NPT obligations by North Korea and Iran, coupled with international inaction, has increased the risk that threatened states will act unilaterally; it also has increased the risk that others might be inclined to pursue the same course, further increasing the likelihood of unilateral military action. It is clear that at least three members of the Security Council may be prepared to consider unilateral action, within their right to use force under Article 51, to deal with these threats preventively. Such an expansion of Article 51 is dangerous—especially in situations where the preventive act might involve two nuclear powers, such as India and Pakistan. Because force is rarely a good option, even with Security Council approval, more reliable, predictable imposition of measures short of force (including sanctions) becomes imperative.

Fourth, *there is a need to address the underlying causes of proliferation,* both to obviate the use of force and to remove the excuses that tend to block international consensus to act when the rules are flouted. Both Indian and Pakistani interlocutors brought to the fore the difficulty of mobilizing support for action, even in clear cases of treaty violation, because the proponents of action had "unclean hands," either because of their own noncompliance or other actions that tended to let the offender off the hook. Here, tools such as *enhanced use of security guarantees* (negative and positive) and *regional security arrangements* would be helpful on both scores (not only to avoid the need to act but also to strengthen legitimacy and effectiveness if action is necessary).

Notes

1. White House, *The National Security Strategy of the United States of America* (September 2002).

2. In a speech at West Point in June 2002, President Bush called for "new thinking" on the preventive use of force. George W. Bush, "Remarks by the President at 2002 Graduation Exercise of the United States Military Academy," June 1, 2002 (www.whitehouse.gov/news/releases/2002/06/20020601-3.html).

3. The need to address this question was highlighted in the report of the UN secretary general's High-Level Panel on Threats, Challenges and Change, *A More Secure World: Our Shared Responsibility* (New York: United Nations, 2004).

4. For a classic, recent statement of this view, see the op-ed by Arthur Schlesinger, "Bush's One Thousand Days," *Washington Post,* April 24, 2006,

p. A17. For an argument that the United States has been more open to the preventive use of force in practice, see Marc Trachtenberg, "The Bush Strategy in Historical Perspective," in *Nuclear Transformation: The New U.S. Nuclear Doctrine,* edited by James Wirtz and Jeffrey Larsen (New York: Palgrave Macmillan, 2005), pp. 9–22.

5. The UN Charter does not define what constitutes a threat to international peace and security; in practice, the members of the Security Council are free to decide this question as they choose. Although the charter refers to actual attack, most, but not all, analysts accept that an imminent attack also falls within Article 51, largely because customary international law has long accepted the use of force in response to an imminent attack. Analysts often especially point to book two of Grotius's 1625 work *De Jure Belli ac Pacis* (*On the Law of War and Peace*). Carefully qualifying the conditions under which an imminent threat justifies the use of force, the book states, "The danger must be immediate, which is one necessary point. Though it must be confessed, that when an assailant seizes any weapon with an apparent intention to kill me I have a right to anticipate and prevent the danger." Hugo Grotius, *On the Law of War and Peace,* translated by A. C. Campbell (Ontario: Batoche Books, 2001), p. 64.

Others point to the Caroline Affair, which involved the 1837 destruction of the American steamer ship *Caroline* (on U.S. territory) by British forces based in Canada. The reason given was self-defense: the British asserted that given the ship's recent history, they anticipated that the steamer would be used to aid Canadian rebels opposing their authority. An exchange of letters took place in 1842 between U.S. secretary of state Daniel Webster and Britain's Lord Ashburton, with Ashburton stating that in the interest of self-defense, "a strong overpowering necessity may arise, when this great principle [respect for the inviolable character of the territory of independent nations] may and must be suspended," and with Webster acknowledging that while "exceptions growing out of the great law of self-defence do exist, those exceptions should be confined to cases in which the 'necessity of that self-defence is instant, overwhelming, and leaving no choice of means, and no moment for deliberation.'" The Avalon Project, Yale University, "Webster-Ashburton Treaty," 1997 (www.yale.edu/lawweb/avalon/diplomacy/britain/br-1842d.htm).

6. For international lawyers, there is a further division of this question into whether the use of force is lawful as well as legitimate. Without unduly disparaging the fine points involved in this distinction, it is not clear how significant this consideration is or should be. If an action is perceived as legitimate, it seems likely that international law will evolve over time to legalize it—at least under customary if not "black letter" international law. Nonetheless, it remains true that some actions may widely be seen as legitimate (the intervention in Kosovo) yet cause considerable debate over whether they are legal (a problem that troubled some of the lawyers from NATO European countries but ultimately proved no barrier to

the decision to act). So for the purposes of this paper, discussion is limited to the legitimacy rather than legality of the action.

There is fairly broad consensus that when the use of force is perceived to be legitimate, it is likely to be more effective in achieving its objectives (at least in the long term), for several reasons. Among these, a legitimate use of force is more likely to gain the cooperation of others and to moderate the costs being imposed on the user.

7. There is an interesting question about whether there should be rules limiting unilateral intervention to support rather than replace a regime. International law has largely accepted that states may call on others to help, for instance, in the case of insurgency. Yet recent history is rife with examples of problems with this approach, from Vietnam to Sri Lanka. The best case is one in which the requesting government is democratically elected and resisting either insurgency or coup; yet in these cases there is likely to be the greatest likelihood of gaining broad international support for military action—as was the case in Haiti.

8. Covert action needs to be distinguished from secret or clandestine action. In the case of covert action, the state denies involvement if the action becomes public; with secret action the state avoids public disclosure but accepts responsibility if the action is revealed.

9. North Korea's plutonium program was effectively suspended, but the regime appears to have proceeded with a clandestine uranium enrichment program.

10. In the case of Libya, some would argue that the Iraqi invasion also implicitly raised a threat of force as part of the mix.

11. G. John Ikenberry and Anne-Marie Slaughter have recently called for the creation of a "concert of democracies" in the final report of the Princeton Project on National Security, *Forging a World under Liberty and Law: U.S. National Security in the 21st Century* (September 2006). See also Ivo Daalder and James Lindsay, "Democracies of the World, Unite," *American Interest* 2, no. 3 (2007): 5–15, and Daalder, chapter 1, in this volume.

12. Of course, the assertion of inherent presidential authority did not begin with President Bush, and in the most important uses of force after September 11, the president has sought and received the support of Congress. But in a number of cases, the president and his principal legal counsel have advocated a view of the "unitary executive" that goes beyond the assertions of his predecessors.

13. Former State Department legal adviser Abe Sofaer has argued in favor of the idea of what might be called "charter-based" interventions to justify the use of force when the Security Council fails to act. Abraham D. Sofaer, "On the Necessity of Pre-emption," *European Journal of International Law* 14, no. 2 (2003): 209–26.

14. Ruth W. Grant and Robert O. Keohane, "Accountability and Abuses of Power in World Politics," *American Political Science Review* 99, no. 1 (February 2005) (www.iilj.org/global_adlaw/documents/GrantKeohanePaper.pdf).

CHAPTER THREE

Military Force against Terrorism: Questions of Legitimacy, Dilemmas of Efficacy

BRUCE W. JENTLESON

I T IS TRUE that terrorism goes way back in history, "as far back as does human conflict itself," as Caleb Carr has written.[1] It also is true that much of the world had been suffering from terrorism for a long time before September 11.[2] Still, the issue did change dramatically after the United States made it its top national security priority and the Bush administration decided on its particular "war on terrorism" approach, with its heavy emphasis on the use of military force.

Among the many issues raised by terrorism, this chapter will focus primarily on two: the legitimacy and the efficacy of the use of military force.[3] As a general matter, questions of norms and legitimacy have greater bearing in the current state of the world than during the cold war, when so much was driven by superpower dominance and competition. While international norms "do not determine action," as Martha Finnemore aptly puts it, they do "create permissive conditions for action."[4] Being able to claim the rightness of action does not just affirm ideals, it also enhances efficacy.

With regard to efficacy, as broadly stated by Gordon Craig and the late Alexander George, "The proposition that force and threats of force are at times a necessary instrument of diplomacy . . . is part of the conventional wisdom of statecraft." History does show that efforts to deal with international conflicts "solely by means of rational persuasion and peaceful diplomacy do not always succeed." Yet "one can also find in history many cases in which threats of force or the actual use of force were often not only ineffective but seriously aggravated disputes."[5]

Based on the regional dialogues that were part of the Brookings Force and Legitimacy project, as well as the growing literature of policy analyses and related studies, five main points can be made.[6] First, spurred in large part by the "September 11 effect," there is a relatively greater degree of international consensus supporting the legitimacy of using force against terrorism than for other objectives—although this consensus is not a full one and has qualifiers and conditions. Second, this consensus on legitimacy is strongest with regard to clear Article 51 self-defense cases and in situations where force is retaliatory; it is weaker with regard to the preemptive use of force and weakest regarding application of force for regime change and other preventive objectives and when substantial civilian casualties are incurred. Third, military strategies for combating terrorism face formidable efficacy challenges. Some of these are matters of doctrine, tactics, and overall strategy stemming from the asymmetric nature of most warfare against terrorists. Other challenges arise due to the problems of sustaining the initial military victory, as demonstrated by events in Iraq, Afghanistan, and Somalia (2006–07); the weaknesses and partially diverging interests of local allies; and tensions between the respective requisites of legitimacy and efficacy. Fourth, the "Iraq effect" has severely undermined the September 11 effect and continues to do so. Fifth, as difficult as these issues have been so far, they are becoming even more so over time.

Legitimacy of the Use of Force against Terrorism

The primary basis for the degree of consensus that does exist internationally comes from the nature of the terrorist threat, which involves non-state actors and extremist states, targets innocent civilians, has catastrophic potential through the use of weapons of mass destruction, and engenders the kind of pervasive fear that can threaten democracy and the very rudiments of civil society. In these respects terrorism's own illegitimacy contributes to the legitimacy of using force against it.

Another key factor is some sense of shared threat across the international community. Some countries did harbor an "it's about time" sentiment, since they had been dealing with terrorism long before the United

States finally made it a priority. However, at least in the immediate aftermath of September 11, the overriding calculation was that with the
United States now in the ballgame, the prospects for dealing effectively
with terrorism were much better.

The U.S. attack on Afghanistan in response to September 11 had a
strong claim to legitimacy. Few questioned the American contention of
acting in self-defense in ways consistent with Article 51 of the UN Charter. The Taliban regime already was under censure and sanctions by the
UN, having been denied Afghanistan's seat in the General Assembly. It
was among the world's worst offenders of human rights and repressors of
women; only two countries in the world had granted it diplomatic recognition. The UN passed resolutions supporting, albeit not explicitly
endorsing, U.S. intervention: UN Security Council resolution 1373 before
the U.S. military action (September 28, 2001), calling on all states to prevent terrorism; resolution 1378 during Operation Enduring Freedom
(November 14), supporting the political process being set up for a new
Afghan government; and resolution 1383 (December 6) supporting the
Bonn agreement establishing the provisional government. NATO invoked
Article V, its collective security provision, to come to the defense of the
United States (the first time in alliance history that Article V had actually
been invoked, ironically in reverse of the prevailing expectation of who
would be coming to the defense of whom). The Organization of American States passed its own supportive resolution. And 170-plus nations
joined the U.S.-led global coalition against terrorism. Some aspects of the
U.S. strategy were debated, particularly the *jus in bello* issues.[7] But the
right to use force in this situation was pretty widely accepted by the international community.[8]

Other U.S. antiterrorist operations, such as the November 2002 surgical missile strike in Yemen that killed six people, including senior al
Qaeda operatives said to be linked to the October 2000 attack on the USS
Cole, while not condoned the way the 2001 Afghanistan invasion was,
also did not set off much outcry at the time. The argument that this, too,
was a retaliatory use of force generally held sway. It also helped that it
was a limited use of force and that the Yemeni government did not object
very much.

But September 11 and Afghanistan have proven to be the exception
more than the rule for a strong consensus supporting the legitimacy of

using force against terrorism. Four main issues have made for more contentious international politics.

THE BUSH DOCTRINE

Whereas the October 2001 invasion of Afghanistan was retaliatory, the "Bush doctrine" claimed the right as well as the need for military preemption. "If we wait for threats to fully materialize, we will have waited too long . . . [O]ur security will require . . . Americans . . . to be ready for preemptive action when necessary to defend our liberty and to defend our lives." The "we" and "our" references were about the unilateral basis for such decisions. Deterrence was dismissed as a cold war doctrine that, however valuable for that era, "means nothing against shadowy terrorist networks with no nations or citizens to defend."[9]

Unilateral preemption posed a much less clear-cut basis for invoking Article 51. States are held to have an inherent right to act in self-defense "if an armed act occurs" and until the UN Security Council acts. Some would extend this to include situations that convincingly meet the criteria for preemption of imminent aggression. The UN High-Level Panel on Threats, Challenges and Change recognized preemptive force as consistent with "long established international law" if it met the fairly restrictive conditions that "the threatened attack is *imminent,* no other means would deflect it and the action is proportionate."[10] If the threat is less imminent and the action thus is preventive, not preemptive, the High-Level Panel stressed coming to the Security Council. This condition reflected assessments of the Bush doctrine as an extension to situations that were not strictly imminent and a preventive use of force.

The unilateral aspect also raised concerns about precedents. As Lawrence Freedman put it, "The ambiguity about situations in which it [military force] might be justified means that elevating this notion [preemption] to a security doctrine rather than an occasional stratagem by the USA creates opportunities for states that might use new-fangled notions of preemption as [a] rationalization when embarking on old-fashioned aggression."[11] If the United States can take preemptive action in the name of its own security and on the basis of its own terrorism threat assessments, then so can other countries: India against Pakistan over Kashmir and Pakistani support for terrorism there, Israel against Hezbollah in Lebanon or against Hamas in the Palestinian territories,

Russia in Chechnya and perhaps its "near abroad." And, as recent events have shown, most of these cases are not hypothetical.

Another case, the Ethiopian intervention in Somalia in December 2006, was accepted to a degree as a legitimate act of preemption. Antiterrorism was not the only factor behind the Ethiopian intervention, but it was one of the major ones both as motivation and justification. The UN Security Council passed two resolutions (1724 and 1725) directly critical of the Islamic Courts government and calling for national reconciliation within Somalia. While including all the usual nods toward sovereignty, the resolutions contained no direct mention let alone criticism of Ethiopia. While the African Union's resolution did not explicitly support the Ethiopian intervention, it did acknowledge "recent positive developments in Somalia which have resulted from Ethiopia's intervention . . . and which has created unprecedented opportunity for lasting peace in the country." The circle was somewhat squared for those concerned about sovereignty by being able to link the Ethiopian action to "the invitation of the legitimate Transitional Federal Government (TFG) of Somalia."[12]

DEFINING TERRORISM

It has proven difficult to craft a definition of what terrorism is and who terrorists are that would be sufficiently consensual yet precise enough to provide a basis for meaningful norms and policies. At the UN the two most contentious issues impeding a common definition have been whether to include states' use of armed forces against civilians and conceptions of the legitimacy of violence, particularly for peoples under foreign occupation. The High-Level Panel report assessed the existing legal and normative framework of the Geneva Conventions and other instruments as sufficient for dealing with war crimes or other such actions by state actors and thus confined the definition of terrorism to nonstate actors. Regarding the second issue, the panel rejected a right of resistance as a justification for terrorism: "There is nothing in the fact of occupation that justified the targeting and killing of civilians."[13] But in its 2005 summit, the UN General Assembly did not agree on either of these two points, largely for political reasons, and thus left the definition issue unsettled.

Other multilateral efforts also have fallen short. The Club de Madrid, formed as a forum and collaborative group in the wake of the March 2004 Madrid train bombings by groups linked to al Qaeda, issued a major statement, "Democratic Response to the Global Terrorist Threat," in its first summit a year later.[14] But for all the declarations, pledges, and recommendations, there was not even a working definition of terrorism. Here, too, it was more politics than linguistics that posed an obstacle.

Another part of the definition issue is, as one of the participants in our Brookings Project put it, the various "my terrorism" problems. Among the examples cited in our African dialogue as terrorism were the threat posed to Rwanda from the Interahamwe (Hutu militia) in refugee camps in the Democratic Republic of the Congo, and the threat posed to Ethiopia from Somali Islamists (this was in July 2006, five months before the Ethiopian invasion of Somalia). In our Middle East dialogue, Israelis expressed their concerns about Hamas and Hezbollah (this in February 2006, four months before the Lebanon war). For China, the terror threat was posed by the Uighurs; for Russia, by the Chechens. It is not just that different states face different threats. Each state's definition of its threats as terrorism can lead to major inconsistencies in what constitutes terrorism, which in turn make for differing policy priorities, as with the small arms trade being a much higher priority than weapons of mass destruction for the terrorist threats much of Africa faces

MORAL HIGH GROUND?

Doubts about claims to the moral high ground also can impede legitimacy. From the start President Bush claimed that the war on terrorism was not just about security but also had higher purposes. Osama bin Laden and the other terrorists were "evildoers." Therefore the goal was to defeat evil and defend freedom: freedom for Afghan women, who had been so brutally repressed by the Taliban; freedom for the Iraqi people, who needed to be liberated from Saddam Hussein; freedom for Americans to live without the fear of terrorist attack; freedom for people everywhere to live without repression and fear. One did not have to lapse into moral equivalence to see how scandals like Abu Ghraib and Guantánamo cut out much of the moral high ground from under the Bush administration. Moreover, the new wave of U.S. global military commitments to governments with horrid human rights records (for example, Pakistan and Uzbekistan) amounted to an "ABT" justification—anybody but terrorists—that has created bedfellows as strange as those engendered by the "ABC"—anybody but communists—rationale used during the cold war.

IRAQ WAR

The effect of the Iraq war on the legitimacy of force as a tool against terror cannot be underestimated. Virtually all discussions of the use of force, especially involving the United States, are that much more contentious because of the U.S. war in Iraq, including the most basic claims to legitimacy in the struggle against terrorism. The assertion that Saddam was significantly linked to al Qaeda was patently rejected by the September 11 Commission as well as by countless other analysts and authorities. This claim was not just the result of flawed intelligence: the case had been made in the inner sanctums of the White House in an intellectually dishonest and politically manipulative fashion. Honest mistakes can hurt one's reputation for competence; deception and manipulation undermine legitimacy. Indeed, there is some sense that U.S. claims of legitimate use of force are subject to even greater skepticism than those of other countries. The recent Somalia case is an interesting example: there was much less outcry over Ethiopia's December 2006 invasion, which involved large numbers of troops and the killing of hundreds of Somalis, than over the U.S. air strikes the following month against an isolated al Qaeda refuge within Somalia.

OTHER APPLICATIONS OF FORCE AGAINST TERRORISM

The United States is not alone in facing international skepticism about its use of force. Russia's justifications for using force against Chechnyan terrorism have not been well received. Israel's claim to the legitimacy of its war against Hezbollah in mid-2006 was hurt by the extensive civilian casualties it inflicted. The initial Israeli attacks against Hezbollah elicited no overt rejection from Jordan, Saudi Arabia, and Egypt. Although these Sunni regimes were principally motivated by self-interest in regard to Hezbollah as a nonstate and radical Shia actor, their stance could be construed as tacit acceptance of the Israeli justification of retaliatory self-defense. But as the war went on and Lebanese civilian casualties mounted, the Sunni states could not countenance any implied legitimation of Israeli action. The fact that Hezbollah helped ratchet up the toll by using civilians as human shields and that it continued to attack Israeli civilians did not suffice to counter the delegitimization of Israel's warfare.

In sum, the legitimacy of the use of force against terrorism was at its zenith in the immediate wake of September 11 and as applied to the invasion of Afghanistan. The claim to legitimacy remains strongest with regard to clear Article 51 cases and situations in which force is retaliatory or limited. Claims of legitimacy have less credence when force is used preemptively and are weakest when force is used for regime change and other preventive objectives and when substantial civilian casualties are incurred. Given this calibrated response, the use of force by the United States to counter terrorism has gone from having the strongest claims to legitimacy to one of the weakest.

Efficacy of Force against Terrorism

To be sure, the overall strategy against terrorism must have political, economic, ideological, and other components. However, while these components are extremely important, they are not the focus of this chapter. Given the nature of the threat and the perpetrators, force must have some role. Al Qaeda's 180-page manual, *Military Studies in the Jihad against the Tyrants,* begins: "The confrontation we are calling for with the apostate regimes does not know Socratic debates . . . Platonic ideals . . . nor Aristotelian diplomacy. But it does know the dialogue of bullets, the ideals of assassination, bombing and destruction, and the diplomacy of the cannon and the machine gun."[15] And, one might add, the message of passenger jets as guided missiles.

Effective use of military force against terrorism, however, has proved problematic in five principal respects. First, the asymmetric nature of military action against terrorists puts regular forces at a distinct disadvantage. Second, initial military victories are often difficult to sustain. Third, local allies on whom external interveners rely often have weaknesses that limit their reliability and have interests that may be in tension with, if not counter to, those of the external party. Tension between the operational requisites of effectiveness and the norms of legitimacy poses a fourth obstacle to effective use of force. Finally, a fifth and compounding impediment to efficacy is the Iraq effect.

ASYMMETRIC WARFARE

The nature of this battle gives terrorists a number of tactical and operational advantages. For all of America's military superiority, terrorists are all too able to target "the soft underbelly of American primacy." They have the "capacity for strategic judo, the turning of the West's strength against itself. . . . Nineteen men from technologically backward societies did not have to rely on homegrown instruments to devastate the Pentagon and World Trade Center. They used computers and modern financial procedures with facility, and they forcibly appropriated the aviation technology of the West and used it as a weapon."[16] This was classic asymmetric warfare: the capacity of the side that is weaker—by the usual measures of military capabilities—to overcome that asymmetry by tactically exploiting the assets it does have to inflict major damage on the militarily "superior" side.

Another aspect of this problem is the intermingling of terrorism and insurgency, which generates the concomitant complexities of combining counterterrorism and counterinsurgency strategies. The Iraq war exemplifies this dynamic and dilemma. Consider the effects at the operational and tactical levels of the insurgents' use of improvised explosive devices (IEDs): not only have they inflicted casualties, but they have also significantly disrupted operations of the American military—indeed, of the entire American presence in Iraq—by requiring a tight lockdown of the Green Zone and making even the road to the Baghdad airport vulnerable.

Another and even more fundamental demonstration of the dangers of asymmetric warfare is how the Bush administration was drawn into the Iraq war as part of the overall war on terrorism. Drawing a stronger opponent into military overextension and repressive blunders is a classic move in asymmetric warfare. It was part of anticolonial strategies in Algeria and elsewhere, and a component of guerrilla warfare against both the United States (Vietnam) and the Soviet Union (Afghanistan) during the cold war era. While it would be an overattribution of strategic savvy to fully credit bin Laden for the Bush administration's blunder into Iraq, goading the United States to further military intervention and occupation in the Islamic world was part of al Qaeda doctrine. Nor was this unique to al Qaeda: provoking a counterreaction that overreaches or misdirects has often been part of terrorists' strategy historically.[17]

Israel also encountered dilemmas of asymmetric warfare in its 2006 conflict with Hezbollah. While planned as a war on terrorism, it proved to be what retired British general Sir Rupert Smith calls "war among the peoples."[18] Unlike al Qaeda, which was based in caves away from population centers, Hezbollah operated from within Lebanese villages, farms, and other locales. They were acting as insurgencies long have, like Mao Zedong's "fish in the sea." And they took it a step further, not just hiding among the people to reduce their own risk but putting many of the civilians at risk by making them their shields. They also fought conventionally, digging in with light artillery. All told, this made them a "hybrid enemy," drawing even further tactical advantages out of the asymmetries and limiting the efficacy of the Israeli military force, despite its technological and numerical superiority.[19]

UNSUSTAINABILITY OF INITIAL MILITARY "VICTORY"

As significant a military victory as Operation Enduring Freedom in Afghanistan seemed in October through December 2001, its sustainability has been much more problematic. Those initial months of military action indeed were impressive. A vast new array of technologies was displayed. Unmanned Predator drones with high-tech sensors and real-time streaming video enabled commanders to direct warplanes to targets around the clock and with unprecedented precision. Special Operations forces infiltrated enemy areas, often riding on horseback in the rugged terrain while technologically equipped to identify targets and communicate the enemy's exact location to bombers overhead. The Taliban regime was ousted; al Qaeda was put on the run. Indeed, looking ahead, one report referred to plans for 2020 or earlier in which "pilotless planes and driverless buggies will direct remote-controlled bombers toward targets; pilotless helicopters will coordinate driverless convoys, and unmanned submarines will clear mines and launch cruise missiles. . . . In years to come, once targets are found, chances are good that they will be destroyed by weapons from pilotless vehicles that distinguish friends from foes without consulting humans."[20]

Within months, though, doubts emerged about the initial military victory's conclusiveness. An FBI-CIA report leaked in June 2002 stated even then "that the war in Afghanistan failed to diminish the threat to the United States. . . . Instead the war might have complicated counterterrorism efforts by dispersing potential attackers across a wider geographic area."[21] A few months later, Lieutenant General Dan McNeil, then U.S. commander in Afghanistan, forecast that it would take up to two more years to eliminate al Qaeda and build an Afghan army strong enough to deny terrorists a future safe haven.[22] Even this proved too optimistic. "The Taliban and Al Qaeda are everywhere," a shopkeeper told an American general in May 2006. "The arrival of large numbers of Taliban in the villages, flush with money and weapons, has dealt a blow to public confidence in the Afghan government, already undermined by lack of tangible progress and frustration with corrupt and ineffective leaders."[23]

In June 2006 U.S. forces launched the largest offensive against the Taliban since the 2001 invasion. NATO, in command of the UN-authorized International Security Assistance Force, also expanded its operations despite being constrained by a number of factors, including many member states' reluctance to commit sufficient troops and to agree to rules of engagement allowing their troops to take on tough and risky fighting. The Afghan army remained of questionable capacity, with only about 27,000 trained soldiers compared to the goal of 70,000. With economic reconstruction and development also proceeding slowly and marked by corruption, and opium production one of the few "booming" sectors of the Afghan economy, the underlying base on which stability must rest also was not secure.[24] One recent assessment showed the number of Taliban attacks had almost tripled from 2005 to 2006, with the prospect at best being the need for "a fully resourced long-term plan to fight a long war."[25]

Another limit to the initial victory in Afghanistan was that while it initially weakened al Qaeda substantially, this gain has since been offset by al Qaeda's adaptations. Its organization has become less unitary and hierarchical and more a networked collection of terrorist groups and even ad hoc cells, what Audrey Kurth Cronin calls "a mutable structure with a strong, even increasing, emphasis on local cells and local initiative."[26] Taking advantage of its refuge in Pakistan, al Qaeda also appears to have rebuilt its central organization.[27]

The recent Ethiopian intervention in Somalia is another example demonstrating the limits of initial military victory. The Ethiopian military removed the Islamic regime quickly while incurring few casualties. It was no contest. The Islamists had seemed militarily powerful when they took over Mogadishu from the warlords in June 2006 but were no match for a real army: Ethiopia's is the strongest in East Africa. But here, too, defeating the adversary militarily has not been sufficient to achieve security and stability in a sustainable way. The Islamists made a tactical retreat to regroup and restrategize for insurgency. The Transitional Federal Government (TFG) was reinstated, but with little if anything done about the root causes of instability, its weakness and dim prospects were apparent within days. The government's call for societal disarmament had to be abandoned almost immediately. There was little reason to think that it would fare better than the thirteen prior efforts since 1991

to create a functioning government. The vicious political cycle that is
Somalia came through in a major clan leader's explanation that he was
not supporting the TFG because "the government is weak. We can't support it."[28] Yet the reason it is weak is precisely because clans like his do
not support it. So the weakness of the government causes the lack of support, and the lack of support causes the government to be weak. By
March 2007 the emboldened Islamists attacked the presidential palace.
Within a month the fighting had become a humanitarian emergency.

In the midst of all this, American Special Operations forces launched
air strikes as part of an operation targeting an al Qaeda cell said to
include leaders of the 1998 embassy bombings. This was the first military
action in Somalia by the United States since its retreat in 1994. That there
was political fallout, setting off anti-American protests that added to the
TFG's problems and further undermined Ethiopia's initial military victory, should hardly have been surprising. Yet two days later a *New York
Times* headline read, "Pentagon Sees Covert Move in Somalia as Blueprint."[29] The ostensible Pentagon evaluation seems puzzling given that
few if any senior al Qaeda operatives had been killed in the strikes and in
light of the negative political reverberations and enhanced prospects of
further statelessness in Somalia.

LOCAL ALLIES: WEAKNESSES AND DIVERGING INTERESTS

The use of force against terrorism often necessitates forging local
alliances. However, such local allies "are often ineffective at fighting
insurgents and can make the problem worse." These allies often have
problematic legitimacy and limited capacity, "hindering the development
of a national strategy, encouraging widespread corruption, alienating the
military from the overall population, and offering the insurgents opportunities to penetrate the military."[30]

During the Afghan intervention, the Northern Alliance, the main anti-
Taliban group, was a valuable ally in many respects, but not in all. As
long as its interests were consonant with those of the United States, it
proved reliable. But when those interests diverged, the Northern Alliance
went its own way. For example, during the key battle at Tora Bora in
December 2001, top al Qaeda leaders including bin Laden managed to
escape, in part because the attacks on the caves were poorly executed by
Northern Alliance fighters. The alliance had already achieved its main
objective—toppling the Taliban. Capturing al Qaeda was less important

to its members, so they were less inclined to run the risks inherent in the
Tora Bora mission. Furthermore, bin Laden and Zawahiri escaped to
Pakistan, where they and al Qaeda found another safe haven—this
despite all the praise of and support for Pakistani president Pervez
Musharraf as a U.S. ally.[31]

Attributing even limited reliability to local U.S. allies in Iraq may be
overstating things. The major debate about the government of Prime Minister Nouri al-Maliki has been whether it is unwilling or unable to fulfill
the role U.S. strategy has assigned it. The biggest problem in creating a
national army and police force has been the stronger loyalties to sectarian
militias. Not one of the major groups—Shia, Sunni, or Kurds—has put
national reconciliation ahead of sectarian advantage. All the talk about
building democracy belies the fundamental problem of the failure to build
the institutional infrastructure necessary for a functioning Iraqi state.[32]

In Somalia the reinstated TFG has proved no more reliable than it was
before being ousted by the Council of Islamic Courts. Other issues
notwithstanding, the Islamic Courts government, during its six months in
power from June to December 2006, had won some support from the
Somali people for "bringing a degree of peace and security unknown to
the south for more than fifteen years. Mogadishu was reunited, weapons
removed from the streets and the port and airport reopened."[33] Yet once
reinstalled by Ethiopian forces, the TFG resorted to its old ways of fac-
tional politics, corruption, and weak governance. As the International
Crisis Group assessed the situation in January 2007, while "Ethiopia's
victory provides an historic opportunity for Somalia's stabilization and
reconstruction . . . it carries equal risks of further instability, protracted
conflict and incubation of extremism. . . . Consolidation of the new situation on the ground depends on the degree to which a legitimate, func-
tional system of governance can be re-established."[34] The International
Crisis Group was leery, although not yet fatalistic, about whether the
TFG was committed to this route.

TENSIONS BETWEEN LEGITIMACY AND EFFICACY

A tension exists between legitimacy and efficacy, between what may be
necessary operationally but could also undermine claims of legitimacy—
which, in turn, could affect efficacy. This has been a frequent problem for
U.S. strategy in Afghanistan and Iraq. One report during Operation
Enduring Freedom, at the height of the war, cited at least ten instances

within six weeks in which commanders believed they had top Taliban and al Qaeda leaders "in [their] cross hairs" but were delayed in getting the necessary attack clearances from U.S. Central Command and the Pentagon for reasons including concern about civilian casualties.[35] At other times clearances came too quickly, as when rifle shots fired in celebration at a wedding ceremony in a small village were mistaken for enemy fire, and the wedding party was bombed, killing a number of people including the bride. Many examples could be cited in Iraq, starting with Abu Ghraib.

Israeli strategy against Palestinian terrorists has encountered this dilemma. Efforts to avoid the collateral damage of civilian deaths and destruction, which undermines claims to legitimacy, have hampered efficacy in hitting targets, as with attempts to assassinate terrorist leaders who embed themselves among civilians. One telling case occurred in September 2003, at the height of the second *intifada* and the Hamas and other suicide bombings. The Israelis had intelligence that senior Hamas leaders—"the 'Who's Who' of Hamas," according to a senior Israeli military official—were gathered in a private home in a densely populated neighborhood in Gaza, one including many children.[36] A key part of the debate was whether to use a quarter- or half-ton bomb, which might not be powerful enough to kill the targets but would avoid the collateral damage of destroying a nearby twelve-story apartment building, or a one-ton bomb, which would be more likely to kill the terrorists but risked the collateral damage. The decision was made to go with a smaller bomb. This choice was made not just with external perceptions of legitimacy in mind but also to accord with Israel's own norms or the "mirror test," as one top Israeli put it: whether, at the end of the day, he could look at himself in the mirror. The quarter-ton bomb hit the house but did not kill the terrorists. "Three moral successes don't equal one operational success," one of the strongest advocates of the larger bomb argued.

IRAQ EFFECT

As the Iraq war has dragged on, it has called into question not just U.S. claims to legitimacy but also American efficacy against terrorism. The metric propounded by Defense Secretary Donald Rumsfeld in an October 2003 memo established the Bush administration's own terms: "Are we capturing, killing or deterring and dissuading more terrorists every day than the madrassas and the radical clerics are recruiting, training and deploying against us?"[37] While these are not the best terms of analysis and assessment, the point here is that the Bush policy comes out net negative even on its own terms. Along with numerous other studies that come to net negative assessments, the administration's own National Intelligence Council concluded that "the Iraq War has become the 'cause celebre' for jihadists, breeding a deep resentment of U.S. involvement in the Muslim world and cultivating supporters for the global jihadist movement."[38]

If there were confidence that working with the United States would make countries safer against terrorism, governments might be more able and willing to work through the legitimacy issue. To be sure, some aspects of American strategy against terrorism have been successful, and there continue to be significant areas of multilateral collaboration. But the net negative assessment, that the overall costs and failures of American and American-led antiterrorism policies are greater than the benefits and gains, is more widely held. That does not bode well for overall strategy against terrorism, let alone for uses of military force.

Looking Ahead

Military force will continue to be essential to strategies against terrorism. Yet in the future it will be at least as difficult, and likely more so, to meet the requisites for both legitimacy and efficacy. September 11 did create a significant degree of international consensus supporting the legitimacy of using force against terrorism. But even that approval was qualified and conditional, with strongest support for use of force in clear Article 51 self-defense cases and instances in which force is retaliatory; support decreased with regard to force used preemptively and was weakest regarding its use for regime change and other preventive objectives and when substantial civilian casualties are incurred. The Iraq war has greatly weakened this degree of consensus, especially for military action taken by the United States. Still, as the invasion of Somalia by Ethiopia demonstrated, there is still some legitimacy attached to acting against terrorist threats, even pre-emptively. The nonrejection by Jordan, Saudi Arabia, and Egypt of the initial Israeli attacks against Hezbollah, even motivated as it was by their own interests and issues, was also significant as a de facto acceptance of the retaliatory self-defense justification for the use of force.

The efficacy challenges for military strategies to combat terrorism are formidable. Even when there have been victories, they have proven difficult to sustain, as exemplified by American experience in Afghanistan and Iraq and probably by the Ethiopian intervention in Somalia. The peace, not just the war, has to be won. This requires much more effective and multifaceted strategies than those used by the Bush administration to fight the global war on terrorism. Military approaches must be based on an understanding that the "revolution in military affairs" in the techno-logical and information arena, however transformational in its own ways, is being significantly countered by asymmetrical and highly political war-fare. The "fish in the sea" strategy of Mao Zedong and the cold war–era communist and nationalist guerrilla strategies have been developed much further by terrorists such as Hezbollah and the resurgent Taliban in Afghanistan. Clausewitz's "war is politics by other means" may never have been truer than it is today.

Some encouragement comes from good work being done by scholars and policy analysts on anti- and counterterrorism strategies, both military and nonmilitary. The initial dismissal of deterrence by the Bush adminis-tration and others is being reassessed.[39] History does show that some ter-rorist movements end without having been defeated militarily, including by losing popular support, unsuccessful generational succession, or tran-sitioning into nonviolent national political processes.[40] Differentiated analyses are helping to better synchronize particular counterstrategies with whatever strategy terrorists are pursuing—for example, by deter-mining when terrorists are using provocation to elicit an overreaction or are using intimidation when they need to exhibit resolve.[41] In addition, to address the rhetoric about the need to get at the "roots" of terrorism, some scholars and policy analysts are assessing the relative importance and dynamics of a range of explanations, including poverty, culture, sociohistorical sense of humiliation, domestic repression, the Israeli-Palestinian conflict, and sociopsychological factors.

U.S. leadership is crucial. Even many critics of the policies pursued by the Bush administration are pushing for *different* rather than *no* U.S. leadership. But right or wrong, fair or unfair, the U.S. intervention in Iraq has generated so much distrust of the United States that it has obscured shared interests and made collective action very difficult. The global com-munity has become skeptical about U.S. claims of legitimacy. Whether that mind-set will change with the next administration remains to be seen. We all lose if it does not.

Notes

The author would like to thank all his colleagues, American and non-American, from the Brookings Project on Force and Legitimacy for such stimulating and informative discussions. Special thanks to Ivo Daalder and Jim Steinberg for their project leadership, Anne Kramer for her invaluable role in the project, Gayle Argon for research assistance, Audrey Kurth Cronin for very helpful comments, and the participants in seminars at the Royal Institute of International Affairs and at the Changing Character of War program at the University of Oxford.

1. Caleb Carr, *The Lessons of Terror* (New York: Random House, 2002), p. 6.

2. There were those who stressed it as a threat to the United States well before September 11. See, for example, National Commission on Terrorism, *Countering the Changing Threat of International Terrorism,* August 2000 (www.gpo.gov/nct); U.S. Commission on National Security in the 21st Century (Hart-Rudman Commission), *Road Map for National Security: Imperative for Change,* January 2001 (www.fas.org/irp/threat/nssg.pdf); and Richard A. Clarke, *Against All Enemies: Inside America's War on Terror* (New York: Free Press, 2004).

3. This caveat is important. The implication here is not that military strategies are the only or even the most important policy components. Moreover, the threats of terrorism from groups within Western societies—which may only have few, if any, links to al Qaeda (for example, some of the recent terrorist acts and plots in Britain)—raise their own distinct sets of issues. See, for example, "Europe's Islamist Terrorism Problem: Challenges and Responses," *IISS Strategic Comments* 12, no. 9 (2006): 1–2.

4. Martha Finnemore, "Constructing Norms of Humanitarian Intervention," in *The Culture of National Security,* edited by Peter J. Katzenstein (Columbia University Press, 1996), p. 158.

5. Gordon A. Craig and Alexander L. George, *Force and Statecraft: Diplomatic Problems of Our Time,* 3rd ed. (New York: Oxford University Press, 1995), p. 258.

6. Note: The Mexico dialogue of the Force and Legitimacy Project did not include an explicit session on terrorism.

7. Adam Roberts, "Counter-Terrorism, Armed Force and the Laws of War," *Survival* 44, no. 1 (2002): 7–32.

8. For an exception, see Thomas M. Franck, "Terrorism and the Right of Self-Defense," *American Journal of International Law* 95, no. 4 (2001): 839–43. Franck cites and responds to a conference of international lawyers, mostly German, held in October 2001, who argued against the legitimacy of the U.S. action in Afghanistan.

9. George W. Bush, "Remarks by the President at 2002 Graduation Exercise of the United States Military Academy," June 1, 2002 (www.whitehouse.gov/news/releases/2002/06/20020601-3.html), pp. 2–3.

10. High-Level Panel on Threats, Challenges and Change, *A More Secure World: Our Shared Responsibility,* December 2004 (www.un.org/secureworld/report.pdf), p. 63 (italics per the original).

11. Lawrence Freedman, *Deterrence* (Cambridge: Polity Press, 2004), p. 4.

12. African Union Assembly, "Decision on Somalia," Eighth African Union Summit, Addis Ababa, January 29–30, 2007 (www.africa-union.org/root/au/index/index.htm).

13. High-Level Panel, *A More Secure World,* pp. 51–52.

14. "Respuesta democratica a la amenaza global del terror," *El Pais,* March 12, 2005, pp. 4–5.

15. Lawrence Wright, *The Looming Tower: Al Qaeda and the Road to 9/11* (New York: Knopf, 2006), p. 302.

16. Richard K. Betts, "The Soft Underbelly of American Primacy," *Political Science Quarterly* 117, no. 1 (2002): 19–36.

17. The author would like to thank Audrey Kurth Cronin on this point.

18. Rupert Smith, *The Utility of Force: The Art of War in the Modern World* (New York: Knopf, 2007).

19. For the "hybrid enemy" characterization, see Eliot Cohen, "The Military Profession and Modern War," Fourth Lee Lecture in Political Science and Government, Oxford University, January 22, 2007.

20. Keith B. Richburg and William Branigan, "Attacks from Out of the Blue," *Washington Post,* November 18, 2001, p. A24; James Dao and Andrew C. Revkin, "A Revolution in Warfare," *New York Times,* April 16, 2002, pp. D1, 4.

21. David Johnston, Don Van Natta Jr., and Judith Miller, "Qaeda's New Links Increase Threats from Global Sites," *New York Times,* June 16, 2002, p. A1.

22. Drew Brown, "Commander: Afghan Missions May Last 2 Years," *Durham Herald-Sun,* September 21, 2002, p. A7.

23. Carlotta Gall, "Taliban Threat Is Said to Grow in Afghan South," *New York Times,* May 3, 2006.

24. Ninety percent of the global opiate supply was coming from Afghanistan. Barnett R. Rubin, "Saving Afghanistan," *Foreign Affairs* 86 (January-February 2007): 57–78.

25. Anthony Cordesman, "Stop Denying the Seriousness of the Afghan Threat," *Financial Times,* January 22, 2007, p. 17.

26. Audrey Kurth Cronin, "How al-Qaida Ends: The Decline and Demise of Terrorist Groups," *International Security* 31, no. 1 (2006): 7–48.

27. Carlotta Gall, "At Border, Signs of Pakistani Role in Al Qaeda Surge," *New York Times,* January 21, 2007; Mark Mazzetti, "Qaeda Rebuilding in Pakistan, Spy Chief Says," *New York Times,* February 28, 2007; and Mark Mazzetti and David Rohde, "The Reach of War: Terror Officials See Qaeda Chiefs Regaining Power," *New York Times,* February 19, 2007.

28. Jeffrey Gettleman, "Clan Politics Dictate the Future of Somalia," *International Herald Tribune,* January 22, 2007 (www.iht.com/articles/2007/01/22/news/somalia.php)

29. Mark Mazzetti, "Pentagon Sees Covert Move in Somalia as Blueprint," *New York Times,* January 13, 2007.

30. Daniel Byman, "Friends Like These: Counterinsurgency and the War on Terrorism," *International Security* 31, no. 2 (2006), pp. 81–82 and 79–115.

31. Gall, "At Border, Signs of Pakistani Role in Al Qaeda Surge;" Mazzetti, "Qaeda Rebuilding in Pakistan;" Mazzetti and Rohde, "Terror Officials See Qaeda Chiefs Regaining Power."

32. Toby L. Dodge, "The Causes of U.S. Failure in Iraq," *Survival* 49, no. 1 (2007): 85–106.

33. International Crisis Group, "Somalia: The Tough Part Is Ahead," Africa Briefing 45 (Brussels, January 26, 2007), p. 1.

34. Ibid., p. 13.

35. Thomas E. Ricks, "Target Approval Delays Cost Air Force Key Hits," *Washington Post,* November 18, 2001, p. A1.

36. This account is drawn from the exceptional article by Laura Blumenfeld, "In Israel, a Divisive Struggle over Targeted Killing," *Washington Post,* August 27, 2006, p. A1.

37. "Rumsfeld's War-on-Terror Memo," *USA Today,* October 16, 2003 (www.usatoday.com/news/washington/executive/rumsfeld-memo.htm).

38. Ken Herman, "White House Releases 'Key Judgments' of Intelligence Findings on Iraq," *Cox Newspapers,* September 29, 2006 (www.coxwashington.com/news/content/reporters/stories/2006/09/29/BC_BUSH_INTELLIGENCE27_COX.html). See also Peter Bergen, "The Iraq Effect: The War in Iraq and Its Impact on the War on Terrorism" (www.newamerica.net/publications/articles/2007/the_iraq_effect_4980); Sharon Burke and Harlan Geer, *The Neo Con: The Bush Defense Record by the Numbers,* September 2006 (www.third-way.com/data/product/file/58/The_Neo_Con_9.5.06_final_electronic_version.pdf).

39. See, for example, Freedman, *Deterrence*; Robert F. Trager and Dessislava P. Zagorcheva, "Deterring Terrorism: It Can Be Done," *International Security* 30, no. 3 (2005–06): 87–123; Caitlin Talmadge, "Deterring a Nuclear 9/11," *Washington Quarterly* 30, no. 2 (2007): 21–34.

40. Cronin, "How al-Qaida Ends."

41. Andrew H. Kydd and Barbara F. Walter, "The Strategies of Terrorism," *International Security* 31, no. 1 (2006): pp. 49–80.

CHAPTER FOUR

The Evolution of Humanitarian Intervention and the Responsibility to Protect

SUSAN E. RICE AND ANDREW J. LOOMIS

I N THE MIDDLE months of 1944, Soviet, British, Chinese, and American statesmen met in Washington to begin to design a postwar architecture that could secure lasting peace. These officials were not quixotic utopians expecting their words on paper to deter future wars. Rather, their deliberations, and those that followed until the June 1945 signing of the UN Charter, presumed that power would remain in the foreground of interstate relations and be shared among strong states. Only by accepting the privileged position of the strong states could the emerging world order generate the coordination necessary to reduce the risk of recurrent major wars. The rules could only be effective to the extent that they were enforced by the strongest states.

The leaders of the Allied nations were realists who focused on national interests, embraced the efficacy of national strength buoyed by military and economic health, and denounced as naïve the view that principles alone could guarantee order. They eschewed Wilsonian idealism and the failed League of Nations. Instead, their views reflected Thomas Hobbes's admonition that "covenants without the sword are but words, and of no strength to secure a man."[1] Thus the system they built was premised on the reality, indeed the utility, of national power.

Human rights were a peripheral consideration in those early days of geopolitics that emerged from the ashes of the Second World War. President

Franklin Roosevelt was more sympathetic to the idea of elevating human rights to a central place in the UN Charter than his British and Soviet counterparts. However, the requirements of political pragmatism, strong resistance from Churchill and Stalin, and Roosevelt's increasing frailty and eventual death in April 1945 conspired to sideline human rights as a core component of the postwar agreement. Respect for national sovereignty and the prohibition of wars of aggression were the twin foundations upon which the nascent UN system was built. Still, human rights did receive brief mention in Article 55, Chapter 9, of the UN Charter, reflecting the Allied powers' judgment that the internal character of the Axis powers had helped fuel Europe's descent into violence.

Only subsequently did the international community begin in earnest to craft a legal architecture that responded directly to the horrors of the Holocaust and the terrible human costs of World War II. On December 9, 1948, the UN General Assembly approved the Convention on the Prevention and Punishment of the Crime of Genocide (Genocide Convention), which defined genocide and made it punishable as a crime under international law. Although the U.S. signed this seminal treaty immediately, and it came into force in 1951, the U.S. Senate did not ratify the Genocide Convention until 1980. The Universal Declaration of Human Rights, unanimously adopted the day after the Genocide Convention by the UN General Assembly, proclaimed the "inherent dignity and . . . the equal and inalienable rights of all members of the human family" and laid the foundation of declared human rights.[2] A raft of subsequent agreements outlawed racial discrimination, torture, and arbitrary detention. Two conventions on economic, social, and cultural rights and on civil and political rights, adopted in 1966, legislated what the Universal Declaration of Human Rights proclaimed. As a new language of rights was being born, the delicate balance began to shift from the inviolability of state sovereignty toward a commitment to protect human welfare.

The ideological conflict of the cold war helped solidify the importance of human rights in the consciousness of western democracies. The ringing language of "freedom versus tyranny" that had been born in opposition to fascism quickly found a second life in the struggle between capitalism and communism, between free and repressive nations. It is no accident that Winston Churchill's famous speech in Fulton, Missouri, in which he coined the term "iron curtain," also warned that ". . . we must never cease to proclaim in fearless tones the great principles of freedom and the rights of man."³ In his inaugural address, President John Kennedy insisted that "the same revolutionary beliefs for which our forbears fought are still at issue around the globe—the belief that the rights of man come not from the generosity of the state, but from the hand of God. . . . Let every nation know, whether it wishes us well or ill, that we shall pay any price . . . to assure the survival and the success of liberty."⁴ The rhetoric of the cold war, reflecting the deeper ideological struggle between east and west, pitted those who respected rights against those who did not. While the action taken by western democracies to uphold human rights lagged behind the high ideals espoused by their leaders, free nations, led by the United States, began to integrate human rights into their foreign policy calculations.

At the same time, a more expansive view of who deserved individual rights slowly percolated into the global public consciousness. New pressures laid waste to the centuries-old system of colonial rule. Fresh sympathies awakened as Jewish émigrés fled Soviet persecution and the abrogation of their religious freedoms. Jim Crow and legally sanctioned discrimination in the United States demanded redress and inspired new thinking about racial inequality at home and the responsibility to uphold human rights abroad.

Amnesty International first convened in 1961 and quickly became a powerful advocate for human rights and humanitarian concerns. Human Rights Watch was launched in 1978, aimed at monitoring the compliance of Eastern European countries with the provisions of the Helsinki Accords. Nongovernmental organizations began to exert their role in ensuring that international organizations and their member states took seriously the responsibility to safeguard human rights.

Mass atrocities in far-flung parts of the world underscored the persistent failure of international law to guarantee the rights and protections to which all people are entitled. After the Khmer Rouge seized power in Cambodia in 1975, nearly 2 million people were killed in the worst genocide since World War II. During his heinous rule of Uganda from 1971 to 1979, Idi Amin presided over the killing of half a million of his countrymen. Vietnamese refugees fleeing their country en masse in shoddy boats, abuses by dictators throughout Central and South America, and the harsh injustices of apartheid South Africa all seared the global public conscience.

The U.S. Congress, reflecting constituent sentiment, began to tackle the question of human rights in the 1970s, first by establishing a human rights bureau in the State Department to monitor and report on human rights abuses abroad. President Jimmy Carter elevated the importance of human rights during his administration. President Ronald Reagan was initially skeptical of the Carter administration's preoccupation with human rights but eventually adopted rights language in supporting democratic freedoms in such places as Central America, Haiti, and the Philippines. Slowly, as a growing consciousness of human rights and freedoms took root, the costs incurred by governments for ignoring their obligations began to mount.

Yet today, more than sixty years since the founding of the United Nations, the foreign policy aim of protecting human rights and democratic freedoms may be newly imperiled. After six decades of the erratic yet eventually inexorable expansion of the concept of human rights, exhaustion with the current war in Iraq has provoked some foreign policy experts to demand a return to a traditional realism. As prominent public intellectual Anatol Lieven recently put it, "We should never launch . . . military interventions simply in response to the urgings of a humanitarian conscience. For while honorable and sincere, these urgings may also prove—as in the wretched case of the eminently well-meaning U.S.-led intervention in Somalia—to be accompanied by a total misunderstanding of the political, social, cultural and military realities of the country concerned, with disastrous results for American prestige and the lives of American and allied soldiers."[5]

Effective application of the principle that all people maintain rights on account of their humanity requires either a world of benign governments or an erosion of the principle of territorial sovereignty. Stanley Hoffmann has argued that a "triple evolution of the idea of human rights"—elementary civil and political freedoms, minority rights, and access to democratic governance—has pressed strongly against the norm of nonintervention.[6] National leaders increasingly contend with a haunting catch-22 that while imposing on another state's internal affairs risks upending the logic of the postwar order, so too does international passivity in the face of systematic abuses of human rights and freedoms.

There is danger in the impulse to submerge liberal ideals beneath the familiar veneer of strategic realism. Since the founding of the Republic, these ideals have been touted as evidence of American greatness. Though the U.S. record is woefully mixed at home and abroad, America has enhanced its image as a benevolent rather than dominating power when it has effectively defended individual liberties and human welfare. Francis Fukuyama bemoans how the Iraq war has wrecked prospects for germinating liberalism in illiberal regimes. He writes that what is needed "is not a return to a narrow realism but rather a *realistic* Wilsonianism that recognizes the importance to world order of what goes on *inside* states."[7] The proposed diminution of human rights and democratic ideals within the panoply of U.S. foreign policy goals runs counter both to American values and American interests. Moreover, it would ignore the plight of millions of people caught each year in ethnic and state-sponsored violence.

As global awareness of human rights and responsibilities grows, it should be matched by renewed calculation of how best to protect innocents from abuse and wanton violence. This analysis should cover not only norms that guide the international community toward action or inaction but also the practical challenges of mustering efficient international action to protect innocent civilians. Understanding both requires a critical evaluation of the practice of humanitarian intervention, which has evolved dramatically over the past two decades. The first part of this chapter provides such an evaluation. The second part of the chapter summarizes the findings of the Brookings Project on Force and Legitimacy and offers recommendations to bolster international will and capacity to construct effective humanitarian interventions when countries fail to fulfill their "responsibility to protect" innocent civilians.

Humanitarian Intervention: 1991–Present

Humanitarian intervention is the armed engagement by outside parties in a sovereign state on behalf of a local population facing an imminent or ongoing violation of their human rights. The increased prominence of humanitarian intervention in U.S. and UN policy is a development with profound implications. While military action to protect innocent civilians continues to be controversial both as a practical and a legal matter, only a few decades ago it was not even deemed a viable option by most national leaders. Today it has become an increasingly frequent feature of international affairs and a prominent purpose of the use of force. Somewhat paradoxically, the first post–cold war incarnation of humanitarian intervention came in the aftermath of a war fought for the explicit aim of defending state sovereignty.

THE GULF WAR

The primary international challenge of the early 1990s dramatized the complexities that states face in straddling the dual responsibility of upholding national sovereignty and protecting human welfare. On August 2, 1990, Iraqi troops crossed the Kuwaiti border in a flagrant violation of Kuwait's sovereignty and territorial integrity. The international community's condemnation came swiftly and firmly. Within twenty-four hours, the UN Security Council demanded that Iraq withdraw from Kuwait immediately and unconditionally. The United Nations passed nine separate resolutions condemning Iraqi conduct before passing UN Security Council Resolution 678 on November 29, which authorized the use of force if Iraq failed to comply with prior resolutions.

The United States worked assiduously to unite international opposition to Iraq's occupation of Kuwait. Secretary of State James Baker traveled to Moscow and throughout the Middle East within six weeks of the Iraqi invasion. President George H.W. Bush invited Iraqi foreign minister Tariq Aziz to Washington and proposed a meeting between Saddam Hussein and Secretary of State Baker in Baghdad. In all their diplomatic maneuvers, the claim consistently advanced by U.S. officials was that if the international community failed to reverse Iraqi incursions into Kuwait, its passivity would imperil the foundations of global order. President Bush and Mikhail Gorbachev, president of the Soviet Union, jointly announced their determination that "aggression cannot and will not pay" at their summit meeting in Helsinki on September 9, 1990.[8] British prime minister Margaret Thatcher stated before the House of Commons on September 6, "If Iraq's aggression were allowed to succeed, no small state could ever feel safe again."[9] The requirement of protecting Kuwaiti citizens was a distant consideration in the calculation of whether to intervene. The widely accepted rationale for this collective response was the importance of enforcing Kuwait's sovereign rights. Western powers formed the tip of a truly international spear in rallying forces and diplomatic support to preserve respect for territorial integrity as the bedrock of international peace and stability.

Yet as the Gulf War drew to a close in early 1991, new concerns arose over the treatment of Iraqi citizens, and the humanitarian imperative to help those imperiled civilians quickly overrode the norm that state sovereignty should remain sacrosanct. Nearly 600,000 Kurds, fleeing the Iraqi army, retreated into the mountains of northern Iraq. By some estimates, as many as 1,000 refugees were dying each day. To address the crisis, the Security Council adopted UN Security Council Resolution (UNSCR) 688, insisting on unfettered access for humanitarian agencies and demanding an end to the repression of civilian populations, "the consequences of which threaten international peace and security in the region."[10]

Respect for Iraqi sovereignty took a back seat during the run-up to UNSCR 688. The military imperatives to liberate Kuwait had already compelled coalition forces to enter Iraqi territory and bomb targets throughout the country. While UN delegates who were not serving on the Security Council did raise the concern that UNSCR 688 represented a direct assault on the concept of state sovereignty, decisionmaking in the UN Security Council was driven by facts on the ground.[11] Self-avowed realist Secretary of State James Baker reportedly telephoned President Bush immediately after a twelve-minute visit to a Kurdish refugee camp and recommended swift humanitarian action.[12] Within days the UN Security Council was at work on the resolution.

With a UN mandate secured, the U.S. government responded quickly. General John Shalikashvili was designated to coordinate the movement of the Kurds from the mountains to refugee camps and ultimately back to their villages. As evidence of the importance that U.S. government officials placed on humanitarian concerns, high officials—notably then chairman of the Joint Chiefs of Staff Colin Powell—rewarded Shalikashvili for his success in managing the operation. His deft handling of the refugee matter was a principal factor in his promotion to Powell's chief aide and in his later selection to succeed Powell as chairman in 1993.[13] U.S. action stood in stark contrast to its inaction three years earlier when reports surfaced that 100,000 Kurds, many of whom were civilians, were systematically killed by Iraqi forces. Following Operation Provide Comfort, the successful operation on behalf of the Kurds, U.S. and allied forces established a Kurdish safe area north of the thirty-sixth parallel and enforced a no-fly zone for twelve years until Saddam Hussein's regime was toppled in 2003.

Operation Provide Comfort was a watershed in two ways. It signaled the displacement of strict conceptions of state sovereignty by the increased urgency to protect human welfare. For the first time in its history, the United Nations mandated a sovereign state to permit humanitarian agencies access to its citizenry. Second, by this action, the UN

Security Council relied on an expansive concept of "international peace and security" to include internal state dynamics in general and forced migration in particular. From 1945 up to Iraq's 1990 invasion of Kuwait, intervention under Chapter 7 of the UN Charter was perceived to be permissible almost exclusively in the case of international aggression. Such aggression served as the original premise for Security Council action over Iraq. With the council's decision to authorize protection of the Kurdish population in northern Iraq, leading states demonstrated a readiness to also embrace human protection as a bedrock principle upon which international peace may depend and which may also require defense by military means. Thus both the protection of national sovereignty and the protection of a civilian population were legitimized as rationale for the use of force within the six-month period of the Gulf War.

Sometimes, however, new norms are slow to establish themselves in the minds of policymakers. On the one hand, top U.S. officials strongly supported action to protect the Kurdish population in northern Iraq. Secretary of State Baker, witnessing the unfolding crisis in April 1991, reportedly said, "We've got to do something—and we've got to do it now."[14] Yet just one year later, as the humanitarian crisis facing the Bosnian Muslims intensified 1,500 miles to the west on the edge of Europe, Secretary Baker famously quipped, "We don't have a dog in this fight."[15] It was a dictum that reflected his realist roots—if U.S. interests were not directly jeopardized by a humanitarian crisis abroad, then the United States had no cause to intervene.

SOMALIA

At the same time as the Kurdish crisis was unfolding, the first Bush administration was grappling with how to handle another acute humanitarian disaster, this one in the Horn of Africa. By the middle of President Bush's final year in office, clans warring in a leadership vacuum had set Somalia ablaze. By September 1992 the International Committee of the Red Cross estimated that as many as 1.5 million Somalis faced imminent starvation, and as many as 5 million more relied on outside assistance for food. Nearly a million people had fled the country.

Congress got out in front of the president on the need to address the crisis. Senators Nancy Kassebaum and Paul Simon held hearings on Somalia and, in late April 1991, urged an immediate cease-fire and relief effort. Simon separately introduced a bill the same month calling for emergency food assistance to be directed to the wider Horn of Africa.

On January 23, 1992, the UN Security Council adopted resolution 733, pressing the secretary general to increase humanitarian assistance in Somalia. In the succeeding months, the UN Security Council passed four separate resolutions calling attention to the conditions of the Somali people, urging a cessation of hostilities and authorizing the first United Nations Operation in Somalia (UNOSOM I) peacekeeping mission to assist in the provision of humanitarian aid.

However, another force was exerting pressure on the White House to do more. By the early 1990s, cable television news had become a staple of the American diet. As President Bush was campaigning for reelection in 1992, pictures of the unfolding crisis were broadcast into American living rooms. Secretary of State Lawrence Eagleburger later acknowledged that "television had a great deal to do with President Bush's decision to go in in the first place . . . very much because of the television pictures of those starving kids."[16] The so-called CNN effect was a phrase coined during this crisis, referring to cable television's ability to galvanize public attention and thus prompt official action over human rights conditions.

Several trends combined to trigger the Bush administration's intervention in Somalia when it was not prepared to act in the Balkans. The administration had confidence that the operation in Somalia would be limited in scope compared to potential military action in Bosnia. Somalia was also viewed as a country devoid of a central government, easing decisions to intervene because the principle of sovereignty was less in jeopardy. National Security Adviser Brent Scowcroft suggested later that acting in Somalia signaled that the United States did not fear military intervention and that it was willing the risk Americans to save Muslim lives, even if it was wary of injecting troops to protect Muslims in former Yugoslavia. "It was not that we were afraid to intervene abroad; it was just that the circumstances weren't right in Bosnia." He added, "For me, Somalia gave us the ability to show they were wrong. It was a Southern Hemisphere state; it was black; it was non-Christian; it was everything that epitomized the Third World."[17] The administration apparently also anticipated a payoff in both domestic and international public opinion if it were seen as defending human welfare and reinforcing respect for human rights. "The opinions of leaders in the Third World matter because to be a 'world leader,' you have to convince people it is in their interest to follow. If everyone hates you, it is hard to be a world leader."[18]

In August 1992 the Bush administration announced it would assist in airlifting Pakistani UN peacekeepers to Somalia to respond to the widespread and acute starvation. Four months later, after much debate and successive resolutions on the intolerable conditions in Somalia, the Security Council passed resolution 794. This resolution identified the conditions in Somalia as a threat to international peace and security, invoked Chapter 7 of the UN Charter, and authorized armed intervention by member states to provide a secure environment for the delivery of humanitarian relief.

American forces entered Somalia on December 8, 1992, as part of the United Task Force, a U.S.-led mission blessed by the UN Security Council with a mandate to provide the security required for relief efforts to proceed. Two days later President Bush informed Congress: "The deployment of U.S. Armed Forces under U.S. command to Somalia as part of this multilateral response to the Resolution (724) is necessary to address a major humanitarian calamity, avert related threats to international peace and security, and protect the safety of Americans and others engaged in relief operations."[19] While casting the motives of the operation in the broadest possible terms—protecting lives, reinforcing regional security, and safeguarding American interests—the primary intention of the Bush administration was to feed and protect an extremely vulnerable population. The forces that President Bush committed were not intended to engage the enemy but rather to provide short-term security for relief efforts and then transfer responsibility to UNOSOM II, the second UN peacekeeping operation.

It was the ultimate outcome of this U.S. intervention that gave humanitarian intervention a black eye in the minds of U.S. policymakers and the American public. As the January 1993 transition from the Bush administration to the Clinton administration took place, a number of factors contributed to a deteriorating situation in Somalia. The U.S. handoff of leadership responsibilities to UN forces was behind schedule. While the transfer of control from U.S. to UN forces was effectively complete by May 1993, the process was dogged by setbacks on the ground. With only 4,000 U.S. troops remaining in Somalia outside the UN chain of command, UN secretary general Boutros Boutros-Ghali pushed for an expanded mandate for UN forces to actively disarm Somali warlords and fighters. UNSCR 814, passed on March 26, 1993, provided this mandate but also made the UN forces into a direct threat to the warlords. Mohammed Aideed, the leading warlord in Mogadishu, began to fight UN forces, killing twenty-four Pakistani peacekeepers on June 5, 1993. In response, the Security Council passed UNSCR 837 on June 6, condemning the attacks, authorizing the arrest and detention of those responsible, and urging member states to contribute military equipment sufficient to deter future attacks. However, raids on UN and U.S. personnel continued, and anti-U.S. ferment spread. The American experience in Somalia ended in tragedy. On October 3, 1993, the infamous Black Hawk Down battle occurred, which claimed the lives of eighteen U.S. servicemen. The image seared in the public mind was of a dead American soldier being dragged ignominiously through the Mogadishu streets as columns of Somalis cheered. The American public was wounded and horrified, as their noble and effective humanitarian sacrifice was repaid with a horrific act of hatred. President Bill Clinton was furious. Congress was outraged, directing much of its ire at the White House. Facing legislation mandating the swift withdrawal of U.S. forces, President Clinton announced that U.S. troops would stop pursuing Aideed and leave the country within six months. Somalia's legacy in the American consciousness was to raise a crippling caution against the armed defense of human rights abroad.

While its legacy for American foreign policy is enduring, Somalia lies sufficiently removed from U.S. soil to prevent it from threatening to swamp the shores of the United States with refugees. Haiti does not.

HAITI

In the late summer months of 1991, just as Congress was beginning to pressure the White House to aid starving Somalis, a coup in Haiti installed a military junta led by Lieutenant General Raoul Cedras. Among other undesirable results, Cedras's repression spurred waves of refugees to take flight for Florida on homemade boats throughout early 1992. Bill Clinton had pounded President Bush on the campaign trail for his immoral policy of turning away Haitians bound for America on the high seas. Anticipating a change of policy, Haitians launched a new wave of boat building when Clinton was elected president in November. This unexpected consequence forced Clinton to reverse course, and upon taking office, Clinton continued the Bush administration's policy of refusing entry of Haitians into Florida. The Clinton administration also moved those rescued at sea to Guantánamo Bay to await repatriation or resettlement elsewhere in the region. At the same time, Clinton applied other pressures on Haiti to allow the ousted, democratically elected President, Jean-Bertrand Aristide, to return to power.

In April 1993 the UN General Assembly voted to establish the International Civilian Mission for Haiti to monitor human rights and provide technical and financial assistance when Aristide returned to the presidency. Two months later the Security Council, acting under Chapter 7, unanimously imposed an international embargo on weapons and petroleum until President Aristide was permitted to return to the presidency. The pressure resulted in a political agreement at Governor's Island in July under which Cedras agreed to relinquish power. After Cedras signed an agreement permitting the return of Aristide by October, the Security Council voted to suspend the sanctions and establish the UN Mission in Haiti (UNMIH).

However, Cedras dragged his feet, and by October he had reneged on the July agreement. The United States sent several hundred American military personnel aboard the USS *Harlan County* to help implement the UN resolution that established the UNMIH. Upon reaching Haiti, only days after the Black Hawk Down trauma, the U.S. ship was greeted at the dock by a band of angry, armed Haitians, who had been whipped into a frenzy by Cedras. In violation of the Governor's Island accords, Cedras's militia opposed any U.S. presence. Ultimately, U.S. forces left Haiti before disembarking. This reversal brought further embarrassment to the U.S. government and was interpreted as a signal that the United States lacked resolve to restore democracy and end the violence in Haiti. The two UN missions were forced out of Haiti, and the Security Council reinstated the embargo.

By July 1994 the international community was fed up with the intransigence of Haiti's leaders and the deplorable human rights conditions. President Clinton ordered the Pentagon to plan for an invasion within the coming two months. Meanwhile, the Security Council adopted resolution 940, authorizing a multinational coalition to "use all necessary means to facilitate the departure from Haiti of the military leadership . . . [and] the prompt return of the legitimately elected President."[20] The resolution asserted that the multinational force would provide a secure environment for the reestablishment of UNMIH to continue its mission. In September, with the Eighty-Second Airborne Division aloft on its way to

Haiti, a U.S. delegation led by former president Jimmy Carter and including Senator Sam Nunn and retired general Colin Powell reached an eleventh-hour agreement with Haiti's military leaders to leave the country and allow Aristide to be restored. The agreement also ended the embargo, retired key military leaders, and paved the way for parliamentary elections. American soldiers landed in Haiti to implement this agreement joined by a twenty-eight-country, 20,000-strong multilateral force.

The period 1991–94 was remarkable for the volume and intensity of challenges foisted upon the international community in a short period time. In a single month during President Clinton's first year in office—October 1993—talks broke down between Iraq and the United Nations over Iraq's responsibility to distribute humanitarian supplies to the Kurds, rioting Somali clansmen killed eighteen servicemen, and a violent Haitian mob dissuaded U.S. forces from disembarking from the USS *Harlan County*.

RWANDA

In the early 1990s, both the principle and practice of effective humanitarian intervention were being put to the test, while the United States and the international community sought improved tools for dealing with a new character of threats. Contending with one more explosion of internal violence threatened to overload a fragile international system that, still in its adolescence, faced successive additional challenges in reconciling the new rules of human rights with the old customs of geopolitical order. Six months after the dark October month in 1993, the system failed altogether.

On April 6, 1994, gunmen shot down the plane carrying Rwandan president Juvénal Habyarimana and his Burundian counterpart. Their munitions brought down both the airplane and the uneasy power-sharing agreement between Hutus and Tutsis that had thinly papered over deep sectarian rifts that had periodically exploded in mass violence in Rwanda and neighboring Burundi as recently as late 1993. This sequence of events initiated one of the most horrific genocides of the twentieth century.

The genocide occurred despite the presence of the United Nations Assistance Mission for Rwanda (UNAMIR), a UN peacekeeping force that had deployed in 1993 to monitor the cease-fire between Rwanda's Hutus and Tutsis. From the outset the force was hobbled by its small numbers and weak mandate. When Major General Romeo Dallaire, commander of the UN forces, learned in January 1994 of a Hutu plot to massacre Tutsi civilians, his pleas to mobilize the peacekeeping force to seize caches of Hutu weapons reportedly met opposition at UN headquarters. Protecting civilians, disarming militants, and choosing sides in the conflict were deemed beyond the scope of UNAMIR's mandate. Recent history had sowed extreme caution in the minds of high UN officials. Iqbal Riza, chief of staff to Secretary General Boutros-Ghali, reportedly said that the consensus opinion of Rwanda held by senior UN officials was "not Somalia again."[21] Then head of UN peacekeeping operations, Kofi Annan later admitted, "You can't look at Rwanda without thinking of what happened in Somalia; in fact, they were happening almost simultaneously."[22]

Two weeks after the start of the killing, with ten Belgian peacekeepers murdered and Belgium and Bangladesh preparing to withdraw the battalions that constituted the backbone of UNAMIR, the Security Council voted to reduce the size of the peacekeeping force from 2,500 to just 270 soldiers and to limit its mandate to monitoring civilians trapped in a stadium and other fixed locations.

In Washington attention shifted away from Rwanda after all embassy staff and most U.S. citizens were evacuated. A week into the crisis, Republican Senate Majority Leader Robert Dole, a forceful voice on ending the violence in Bosnia, said on a Sunday news program, "I don't think we have any national interest here. I hope we don't get involved there. I don't think we will. The Americans are out. As far as I'm concerned in Rwanda, that ought to be the end of it."[23] While there were some words of alarm expressed by members of Congress, no one called for the insertion of U.S. troops. Ten weeks into the killing, Representative Alcee Hastings offered from the floor, "Condemn the genocide, and maybe we can motivate the world and the United Nations."[24] With respect to the family of congressional concerns, Rwanda was largely an orphan.

Meanwhile, senior administration officials continued to struggle with competing crises. National Security Adviser Anthony Lake later said, "I was obsessed with Haiti and Bosnia during that period, so Rwanda was . . . a 'sideshow,' but not even a sideshow—a no-show."[25] The administration waited weeks, as it debated internally, before condemning the killing as genocide. Although news coverage of the Hutu onslaught eventually intensified, there was little appreciation initially of the scale of the killing. Few practical ideas emanated from New York or Washington on how to stop the violence, and the editorial pages of the major newspapers leveled little criticism at U.S. and UN inaction.

Arguably, the greatest fault of the international community was its failure even to contemplate humanitarian intervention to stop the genocide. No government acted to end the killing. No one in the U.S. government formally proposed the dispatch of U.S. forces to Rwanda. As the genocide unfolded, Washington held no high-level meetings in which Rwanda formed the heart of the agenda.

The killing began a mere week after the last U.S. forces had withdrawn from Somalia, and official Washington was eager to turn its attention away from Africa. As in New York, the shadow of Somalia dimmed the imagination of U.S. policymakers, Congress, and the press alike. In the first few weeks, Washington failed to grasp the true gravity of what was transpiring—a genocide, not another spasm of violence. Thereafter, Washington, the UN, and the rest of the international community failed to consider, much less launch, any humanitarian intervention in a time frame that could have halted the genocide.

The Rwandan Armed Forces and Interahamwe militia continued killing for some 100 days. By the time the violence waned, an estimated 800,000 Tutsis and moderate Hutus had been murdered, mostly by mobs of Hutu youth wielding machetes and knives. The onslaught ended by the middle of July 1994, when forces from the Rwandan Patriotic Front entered the country from Uganda, seized the capital, Kigali, and drove out the Hutu genocidaires.

When the French government sought UN Security Council approval to intervene in Rwanda under Operation Turquoise, Washington dared not object—chagrined, if not motivated, by its own inaction. Senior U.S. officials, accustomed to largely cooperative relations with France, failed to adequately question French motives. As a consequence the international community committed yet another sin of omission—allowing France, with its close historic ties to the Hutu leadership, to provide protection to the perpetrators of genocide as they fled alongside refugees into neighboring Zaire.

Only then, when faced with yet another massive humanitarian crisis, did the United States decide to deploy forces. In July 1994 the U.S. government finally mobilized its forces to assist the million refugees crammed into unsanitary, cholera-prone camps. At the height of the relief operation,

2,600 U.S. troops from various points in East Africa contributed to the effort. Regrettably, these forces were employed, albeit with the best of intentions, not to shield the victims of genocide (as it was too late to do so) but instead to shelter and water another set of desperates—the perpetrators of genocide, their sympathizers, and the refugees that they used as human shields.

BOSNIA

The Bosnian crisis, which began three years before the Rwandan genocide and continued for a year after its completion, commanded a great deal more international attention. Tensions between ethnolinguistic groups in Yugoslavia had been muted under the firm hand of Tito, who from 1945 until his death in 1980 curtailed expressions of ethnic nationalism. After Tito a weak constitution worked against the consolidation of a strong central government. This arrangement allowed political opportunists to exploit ethnic divisions and use propaganda to build power among their respective ethnic kin.

The most notorious perpetrator was Slobodan Milosevic, who ascended to the presidency of Serbia in 1989. He had secured strong grassroots support by brashly defending minority Serbs in the heavily Albanian-populated Serb province of Kosovo. His strong pro-Serbian nationalist rhetoric sent tremors throughout Yugoslavia. Anxieties were particularly acute in those ethnically mixed republics in which nationalist passions had been kept at bay by a mixture of strategies involving both repression and the delicate fostering of a civic (Yugoslav) identity. The most endangered of these republics was the most heterogeneous—Bosnia-Herzegovina.

The same year Milosevic took the presidency, Warren Zimmermann was newly appointed as U.S. ambassador to Yugoslavia. He had a strong record as an advocate of human rights, having led the U.S. delegation to the Review Conference of Helsinki signatory states that aimed to advance human rights concerns in the Soviet Union and its satellite states. Ambassador Zimmermann took a new message to the Yugoslav leaders when he made his introductory calls in Belgrade. Although human rights concerns had not been prioritized by Washington during the cold war, Yugoslavia's "failures in the human rights area . . . now loomed larger." The U.S. government was insistent that the unity of the country had to be consistent with Yugoslavia's "progress toward democracy."[26]

Yet the rights of ethnic minorities in parts of Yugoslavia already were under assault. Two years later, with growing anxiety throughout Yugoslavia about ethnic-based violence and Serbian repression, the country began to unravel. On June 25, 1991, Slovenia and Croatia declared their independence from Yugoslavia. After a cascade of events, including a punishing war between Serb-dominated Yugoslavia and Croatia, the leaders of ethnically diverse Bosnia-Herzegovina announced plans for Bosnia's separation from the remainder of Yugoslavia. Given the substantial Serb and Croat populations in Bosnia, the call for independence triggered all-out war over Bosnian territory. Serb and Croat troops clashed in Bosnia, while Serb forces were particularly aggressive in assailing the Bosnian Muslim population to carve out territory for their fellow Serbs.

As news began to flow from the Balkans, western media outlets vividly reported repression of Bosnian Muslim and Croat populations by Bosnian Serb officials as well as details of forcible relocation, widespread rape and violence, and extensive killing by the Serbian military. Human rights organizations bravely documented the descent into savagery. Nonetheless, two influential publications both reflected and helped justify the initial hesitation that prevailed among U.S. officials in the early years of the Bosnian war. Samuel Huntington, in his famous 1993 *Foreign Affairs* article "Clash of Civilizations," argued that warfare on the horizon would take place across ethnic, religious, and linguistic fault lines rather than along political or ideological divisions as in the past.[27] Published the same year was Robert Kaplan's *Balkan Ghosts,* which claimed that "ancient ethnic hatreds" were the principal source of violence in southeast Europe.[28] Both pieces were grounded in the assumption that ethnic homogeneity existed in conflicting communities. The theses also rested on the notion of endemic interethnic animosity and failed to account for the critical role of demagogues who fuel interethnic hostility for personal gain. In effect, these works suggested that if such ethnic hatreds had plagued the region for centuries, it would be folly to attempt to resolve these during a short period of history with something as brief as an outside intervention. Early in the trajectory of the Bosnian war, Defense Secretary Dick Cheney declared on CNN, "It's tragic, but the Balkans have been a hotbed of conflict . . . for centuries."[29] President Bush cast the war as the result of "age-old animosities . . . century-old feuds."[30]

At the United Nations in late 1991, officials deflected calls for an armed intervention to stop the bloodshed. While Lord Peter Carrington, acting on behalf of the European Community, attempted to develop a peace plan, outgoing UN secretary general Javier Pérez de Cuéllar dispatched former U.S. secretary of state Cyrus Vance to the region. An advantage that Vance had over Carrington was that he could offer a UN peacekeeping force, and he brokered an agreement that provided for the withdrawal of Serb forces from Croatia. The UN Protection Force (UNPROFOR) was deployed to southern Croatia to reinforce the peace agreement by separating Serb and Croat forces. As the fighting intensified in Bosnia, UNPROFOR's mandate gradually expanded—first to the delivery of humanitarian supplies and protection of released civilian prisoners and then to monitor Serbian compliance with the UN no-fly zone over Bosnia. The Security Council failed, however, to authorize an increase in force levels sufficient to carry out the expanding mandate.

At the same time, the incoming UN secretary general Boutros-Ghali reportedly maintained that "Yugoslavia is a European problem. Let the Europeans deal with it."[31] This attitude, combined with the member states' lack of resolve to forcefully confront the ethnic violence, established a pattern, arguably, of well-intentioned passivity regarding the problem of Serbian aggression.

Humanitarian efforts continued, but Western officials remained reluctant to employ military force. In July 1992 Sadako Ogata, UN High Commissioner for Refugees, advanced a response plan. The objectives were respect for human rights and humanitarian law, preventive protection, humanitarian access to those in need, measures to meet special humanitarian needs, temporary protection measures, material assistance, and repair and rehabilitation.[32] One month later the Security Council called for "all measures necessary" to ensure that humanitarian supplies were delivered to Bosnia.[33]

Bush administration officials were uninterested in a military option in 1991 and 1992. Secretary of State Baker announced his preference for Europe to solve the problem. Deputy Secretary of State Lawrence Eagleburger, a former ambassador to Yugoslavia, struck a defeatist chord: "The tragedy is not something that can be settled from outside and it's about damn well time that everybody understood that. . . . There is nothing the outside world can do about it."[34]

After the administration transitioned from Bush to Clinton, there was greater receptivity to lower-level officials' proposals for the use of force. Still, the new administration was also initially reluctant to implement such options. Yet as the genocide in Bosnia persisted, pressure for military intervention continued to mount, including from some in Congress. Polls also revealed a growing public concern with perceptions that a history of genocide in Europe was repeating itself. In May 1993 Secretary of State Warren Christopher went to Europe to consult on, rather than to sell forcefully, a new policy coined "lift and strike"—lift the arms embargo and strike the Serb forces. Europeans responded frostily to the proposal, not least because their peacekeeping forces might be caught in the middle, and lift and strike was shelved.

Then in June 1995 news of a massacre by Serb forces at Srebrenica sent shock waves through U.S. and European publics, as it crystallized the dual perception of Serbian malevolence and UN impotence. Serb general Ratko Mladic and his forces seized the so-called UN safe area ("protected" by lightly armed UNPROFOR troops) and slaughtered as many as 7,400 Muslims. Reports that Serb forces were separating the draft-age men from the women, children, and elderly, and that large numbers of men had disappeared underscored the genocidal character of the killing.

With increased public attention, congressional pressure, allied support, as well as a successful Croatian offensive against Serb forces in eastern Croatia all converging, the Clinton administration—spurred by National Security Adviser Anthony Lake and UN Ambassador Madeleine Albright—decided to take bold action to end the violence in Bosnia. Clinton dispatched Lake to shuttle across Europe to build support for an invigorated policy through an intense series of negotiations, backed by the threat to use force if a negotiated solution proved unattainable. Lake's efforts were bolstered by tragedy when on August 28, 1995, a Bosnian Serb shell exploded in a Sarajevo marketplace, killing several dozen people. International attention and Western resolve had already begun to converge, and this final act of defiance of U.S., European, and UN calls for restraint triggered NATO air strikes, starting August 30, that targeted Bosnian Serb installations near Sarajevo. Combining the air strikes with invigorated diplomatic efforts proved to be the right combination to end the war.

On November 21, 1995, after twenty days of negotiations spearheaded by U.S. Assistant Secretary of State Richard Holbrooke at the Wright-Patterson Air Force Base in Dayton, Ohio, the presidents of Croatia, Yugoslavia, and Bosnia signed the peace accord ending the war in Bosnia. Yet, in spite of all the delicate issues resolved in the peace talks, the issue of the status of Kosovo remained unsettled. It would later become the issue that would prompt the fullest expression of President Clinton's readiness to use military force to save lives.

KOSOVO

In the semiautonomous province of Kosovo in southern Yugoslavia, the Albanian community, which constituted 90 percent of the population, had little effective political power. Polemical counterclaims over competing ancestral histories and territorial affiliation were fiercely levied by the Albanian and minority Serb populations. Kosovo was contested land, a flash point for largely dormant Serb and Albanian animosities.

In 1989 the Serbian Assembly under the direction of Milosevic effectively stripped Kosovo of its autonomous status, initiating increased repression and violence. In March 1998 a few hundred Albanian Kosovo Liberation Army insurgents assembled to seek redress of their claims. By July, incited by claims of Serb oppression, the Kosovo Liberation Army had grown to several thousand.[35] Humanitarian conditions for the Muslim Kosovar Albanians worsened.

Despite concessions by Milosevic in a series of high-level diplomatic efforts in the fall of 1998 and early spring of 1999, nearly 80,000 Albanians were forced by Serb forces to flee their homes between the end of December and mid-March 1999.[36] On March 24, 1999, NATO launched Operation Allied Force to halt the violence against Albanian civilians and to arrest the further decay of humanitarian conditions in Kosovo. The NATO-led bombing campaign continued until June 11, 1999, when Milosevic relented, agreeing to end all violence in Kosovo, withdraw all Serb forces, and submit to an international presence under UN auspices. Authorized under Chapter 7 of the UN Charter, the UN would oversee a process to establish a semblance of self-government and enhance economic and political conditions in the region. NATO swiftly deployed a force to Kosovo to provide security. A complementary UN civilian mission remains to assist refugees and displaced persons, help maintain law and order, and protect human rights.

The Kosovo bombing campaign was highly controversial because it was launched by NATO without UN Security Council authorization. While the United States and its European partners sought, and would have strongly preferred, such authorization, the prospect of a Russian and perhaps a Chinese veto dissuaded them from pressing for a Security Council vote explicitly authorizing the use of force. Officials in Western governments felt that their cause was just, and a vote in the Security Council was not essential for them to act. NATO blessing, they maintained, would suffice. They cited a long series of UN resolutions challenging Serbian treatment of the Albanian population in Kosovo, in particular UNSCR 1199, approved on September 23, 1998, by a vote of 14-0, which called for the immediate withdrawal of Serbian forces from Kosovo. The same resolution referenced Chapter 7 of the UN Charter, which allows for enforcement action to maintain international peace and security.[37] U.S. officials heralded this resolution as legal justification for the use of force and thus bypassed the unambiguous legitimization that an explicit Security Council authorization would have provided.

The lack of UN support complicated but ultimately did not preclude U.S. efforts to gain European leaders' agreement to confront Serbian forces militarily. While most NATO countries have long argued that a Security Council mandate was required for offensive military force to be legally authorized, in the end the humanitarian conditions in Kosovo persuaded European states to join in the effort to protect civilians.

French president Jacques Chirac argued that military force was justified in the face of a humanitarian crisis: "In this particular case, we have a resolution which does open the way to the possibility of military action. I would add, and repeat, that the humanitarian situation constitutes a ground that can justify an exception to a rule. . . . France would not hesitate to join those who would like to intervene in order to assist those who are in danger."[38]

On October 6, 1998, French foreign minister Hubert Védrine and Italian prime minister Romano Prodi together stated that "our shared position of principle . . . is that, before any military intervention . . . the Security Council must adopt a Resolution authorizing that intervention. But in the specific case of Kosovo, on which a Resolution citing Chapter VII has already been adopted, we must . . . keep a very close eye on the humanitarian aspect of the situation . . . which can demand very rapid . . . implementation of measures to deal with an emergency."[39]

British prime minister Tony Blair was as forthright as any allied leader in his insistence that intervention was morally justified and that Milosevic must answer for the war crimes committed under his direction. "There are no half-measures to his brutality, and there can be no half-measures about how we deal with it. No compromise, no fudge, no half-baked deals," he said in making the case for joining the U.S.-led military intervention. Blair later defended U.S. leadership, saying "America has once again shown that it has the vision to see that instability, chaos and racial genocide in the heart of Europe will never affect Europe alone."[40]

Even German chancellor Gerhard Schröder faithfully supported the air war. It was the first time the German military participated in combat since the Second World War.

United Nations Secretary General Kofi Annan contributed to the sense that the humanitarian norm of protecting human lives had outpaced the norm of sovereign inviolability. Although he asserted that the UN Security Council was solely responsible for authorizing nondefensive military force, he also acknowledged that "there are times when the use of force may be legitimate in the pursuit of peace."[41]

The Independent International Commission on Kosovo, initiated by Swedish prime minister Göran Persson and endorsed by Secretary General Annan, found that the U.S.-led war in Kosovo was "illegal but legitimate."[42] The finding held that despite circumventing the Security Council, NATO answered a growing humanitarian disaster, a function that the UN Security Council was unable to fulfill. "The intervention was justified," the commission found, "because all diplomatic avenues had been exhausted and because the intervention had the effect of liberating the majority population of Kosovo from a long period of oppression under Serbian rule."[43] NATO violated the letter of the law but acted in accordance with the spirit of the UN Charter.[44]

For the principle of human rights and the practice of humanitarian intervention, Kosovo was a crowning moment. In Kosovo states risked the charge of illegality in pursuit of what they deemed legitimate humanitarian imperatives. At the time many UN member states vigorously protested NATO action in Kosovo. However, after the military campaign ended, the UN Security Council passed resolution 1244 that, in effect, legalized NATO action retroactively.

DARFUR

While the United States led decisive intervention in Kosovo, which was retroactively endorsed by the international community, the process was not a harbinger of things to come. Nowhere is this more evident than in

Darfur. Massive crimes against humanity, perpetrated by the government of Sudan and its Janjaweed militia, started in 2003 and persist in 2007. The U.S. government has rightly termed these crimes "genocide" while the UN and others prefer to call them "crimes" or "atrocities." Terminology aside, the facts remain: as many as 450,000 have been killed and 2.5 million displaced or rendered refugees. Khartoum-sponsored violence has spilled over into Chad and the Central African Republic, threatening thousands more civilians and destabilizing fragile neighboring governments.

There can be little doubt that the scale of atrocities in Darfur surpasses any reasonable interpretation of the threshold for action contemplated under the "responsibility to protect." Yet the international community has failed over a period of four years to halt the killing. China and Russia have chilled any efforts at meaningful sanctions. A U.S.- and Nigerian-brokered peace agreement, signed in May 2006 by only one of the three Darfuri groups rebelling against the Sudanese government, was doomed from the start. Violence has only increased since the Darfur Peace Agreement was signed. Indeed, subsequent to the agreement, Khartoum launched successive massive offensives against civilians in Darfur—in effect, a second wave of genocide.

To its credit, in 2004 the nascent African Union (AU) deployed a force that reached almost 7,000. Its mandate was to report on cease-fire violations, "assist in the process of confidence building," and "contribute to a secure environment" so that humanitarian relief could be delivered and internally displaced persons and refugees could return home.[45] While it has been the only international actor willing to face bullets to save civilians in Darfur, the undermanned, underresourced AU force has been consistently hobbled by a weak mandate and inadequate logistical and financial support, despite contributions from NATO and Western governments. In 2006 the AU finally acknowledged the obvious: it is unable by itself to secure hundreds of thousands at risk across an area the size of France. The African Union called for an enlarged UN force to replace it, and the UN Security Council passed resolution 1706 in August 2006, authorizing the deployment of a robust 22,000-person force with a Chapter 7 mandate.

The force has not deployed, however, because the government of Sudan has refused to permit it. In September 2006 Sudan agreed to allow the AU to remain under an extended mandate. Shortly thereafter, the

United States threatened an unspecified confrontation with Khartoum should it continue to resist a UN force. However, instead of following through on that threat, the United States, UN, African Union, China, and European countries agreed in November to establish a "hybrid" UN-AU force, as the third in a three-stage process to gradually introduce UN elements into Darfur. The concept of a hybrid force came into existence in an effort to win Khartoum's assent to the deployment of more troops. The hybrid force is to be financed by the UN and enjoy UN logistical support. The troops, the secretary general's special representative for Sudan, and the force commander (appointed jointly by the UN and AU) are all to come from Africa, if possible. The command and control arrangements are muddied in a manner reminiscent of UNPROFOR–NATO "dual key" arrangement that failed in Bosnia. Finally, the hybrid force is to operate under a (presumably weaker) mandate derived from the AU rather than the UN and will consist of a substantially smaller contingent than originally envisioned (17,000 versus 22,000). In short, the hybrid arrangement falls far short of the measures that the Security Council approved in resolution 1706 to protect civilians in Darfur.

However, the Sudanese government has refused to accept the hybrid force. The United States threatened in November 2006 to resort to "plan B"—punitive steps against Khartoum—if by December 31, 2006, the Sudanese government did not stop attacks against civilians in Darfur and agree unequivocally to the UN-AU hybrid force. The government of Sudan did not take either step, but there is no indication that the United States will resort to plan B. The net result is that for four years the perpetrators of genocide have been allowed to veto effective international action to stop it. This tragic situation highlights the dilemmas of respecting state sovereignty versus violating state sovereignty in order to protect the innocent.

International Norms and the Responsibility to Protect

The evolution of humanitarian intervention has occurred in stages. During the Gulf War, the Security Council's requirement that Iraqi leaders permit access to humanitarian agencies was a pivotal point in the international community's commitment to human welfare. Subsequently, UN member states increasingly accepted the premise that internal strife, including the abuse of human rights within sovereign boundaries, can fuel large-scale civil conflict. Civil wars, in turn, often spill over to undermine regional or international peace and security. The UN Security Council's actions on the basis of this recognition effectively broadened the definition of permissible uses of force under Chapter 7 of the UN Charter. Representative of this trend over the last fifteen years are the UN-led or -blessed interventions in Bosnia, Haiti, Sierra Leone, Liberia, East Timor, and the Democratic Republic of the Congo—all under Chapter 7 of the UN Charter. A notable, final leap was the willingness of states to use military force in Kosovo on behalf of foreign nationals absent an explicit Security Council mandate. After a decade of difficult decisions as to whether or not to intervene to save civilians, at the start of the twenty-first century, international attention turned to how and when to combat atrocities.

While imperfect interpretations of historical experience, moral necessity, and military capability had been the primary guidelines for policy throughout the 1990s, the international community craved a new set of normative guidelines that could shape action and guide decisionmaking in the future. Toward this end the International Commission on Intervention and State Sovereignty (ICISS), cochaired by Gareth Evans and Mohamed Sahnoun, launched the international normative debate over this issue in earnest in December 2001 when it released a comprehensive and groundbreaking report entitled *The Responsibility to Protect*.[46] This report was commissioned by the government of Canada and reflected the consensus of a diverse group of international statesmen. Its principal conclusion was that national sovereignty, while vitally important, is neither inviolable nor a legitimate justification for inaction by the international community when sovereign governments are unwilling or unable to protect their citizens from large-scale violations of human rights, crimes against humanity, ethnic cleansing, or genocide. The ICISS stressed that the foremost responsibility to protect citizens of a nation lies with the government of that nation. However, when governments cannot do so, or when governments themselves perpetrate massive human rights abuses, then the international community can and should act forcefully—as a last resort—when peaceful means have failed, using minimal necessary force and, ideally, with UN Security Council blessing. The commission defined the "responsibility to protect" (now frequently referred to as "R2P") as comprising three elements: first, the "responsibility to prevent" violence against civilians by addressing the causes of conflict through peaceful means such as development and diplomacy; second, the "responsibility to react" to massive abuses through diplomacy, sanctions, and, in extremis, military intervention to halt abuses; and third, the "responsibility to rebuild" in the wake of conflict and, especially, international intervention.

In addition, the ICISS addressed the crucial question of whether military action to halt atrocities can be deemed legitimate without Security Council approval. It concluded that council authorization is the gold standard of legitimacy and should be sought in all instances. Absent this authorization, the ICISS recommended three alternatives. The second-best option, in lieu of a Security Council mandate, would be UN General Assembly approval in emergency session under the Uniting for Peace procedure, as used in the case of the Korean War. If this fails, action should be taken under the jurisdiction of a relevant regional organization under Chapter 8 of the UN Charter, with Security Council approval sought subsequently. Finally, the ICISS acknowledged that if the Security Council neglected to act "in conscience-shocking situations . . . concerned states may not rule out other means to meet the gravity and urgency of that situation—and that the stature and credibility of the United Nations may suffer thereby."[47]

After the release of the ICISS report, the international normative and legal framework evolved. The debacle in Iraq and the ongoing genocide in Darfur added urgency to the conversation as U.S., UN, and international policymakers wrestled with the question: *When, and under what circumstances, is it legitimate for outsiders to use force to address a humanitarian crisis in a sovereign state?* In December 2004 the UN secretary general's High-Level Panel on Threats, Challenges and Change endorsed the emerging norm that "there is a collective international responsibility to protect, exercisable by the Security Council authorizing military intervention as a last resort, in the event of genocide and other large-scale killing."[48] However, it did not tackle the question of what to do when the Security Council does not act. Subsequently, in May 2005 UN secretary general Kofi Annan issued his own report, *In Larger Freedom,* which responded to his High-Level Panel and set the stage for the upcoming UN sixtieth anniversary summit.[49] Annan argued that the challenge was not to find alternatives to the Security Council but to make the council work better. He recommended that the Security Council adopt a resolution setting out the main principles as to when and how to use force to protect civilians, drawing substantially on the criteria put forth by the ICISS, and commit to observe these principles in future decisionmaking.

The UN Summit Declaration of 2005 adopted by the General Assembly affirmed that the UN has the responsibility to protect populations from genocide, war crimes, ethnic cleansing, and crimes against humanity. Further, member states agreed, "We are prepared to take collective action, in a timely and decisive manner, through the Security Council, in accordance with the Charter, including Chapter VII, on a case-by-case basis and in cooperation with relevant regional organizations as appropriate, should peaceful means be inadequate and national authorities are manifestly failing to protect their populations."[50] In April 2006 the UN Security Council reaffirmed this statement, giving it additional weight under international law in resolution 1674.

How Others See It

In order to illuminate the nuanced attitudes that will shape and ultimately guide international action or inaction with respect to the responsibility to protect, the Brookings Institution convened a series of regionally based roundtable discussions on the theory and application of the concept. The ICISS report provided the starting point for these dialogues, which occurred between February 2004 and July 2006. Participants included experts from the United States, Europe, Mexico, China, South Asia, the Middle East, and Africa. While conversations with small groups of experts cannot be extrapolated to serve as indicators of entire national attitudes, the conversations do shed light on how policy elites in different countries approach the responsibility to protect. Most international interlocutors embraced R2P, at least in principle; however, they differed substantially over its importance, urgency, appropriate threshold for action, and whether prior UN Security Council approval of intervention was necessary.

The U.S. participants in these dialogues strongly and unanimously subscribed to the norm of the responsibility to protect. They took the view that the international community has the right, and some insisted the obligation, to act in the face of massive violations of human rights, using force if necessary. They lauded Kosovo as a precedent for action when the UN fails to respond and lamented U.S. and international paralysis over Darfur. In the case of Darfur, as with Rwanda, American participants viewed the practical constraints on international action as a function of the lack of political will and, to a lesser extent, of high-caliber African military capacity to conduct enforcement actions. Though American participants strongly preferred that any international humanitarian intervention win Security Council approval, they did not view international law or lack of legitimacy as binding constraints on actions taken by the United States or others. In particular, they were prepared to seek alternative means of legitimizing potential interventions—whether endorsement by a relevant or concerned regional organization, an ad hoc coalition, or ex post facto Security Council legitimization. U.S. participants recognized that retroactive U.S. effort to justify, at least partially, the invasion of Iraq on humanitarian grounds complicates perceptions of America's motives in places like Darfur. Still, the American discussants remained fully committed to the R2P norm and viewed the Security Council's failure to stop the genocide in Darfur as another blot on the UN's record, which even the most charitable members of the group perceived as mixed.

African participants professed an unyielding determination to apply the responsibility to protect effectively. They noted that humanitarian challenges related to the responsibility to protect mainly manifest themselves in Africa and cost thousands of African lives. They lauded the new African Union charter for explicitly rejecting the doctrine of the inviolability of sovereign states adopted by its predecessor, the Organization of African Unity. For Africa the major constraint on effective action is neither law nor legitimacy nor lack of political will; it is insufficient African resources and capacity to execute effective enforcement action without major external support. Generous African commitments to various UN and regional operations have absorbed most excess peacekeeping capacity on the continent. The lack of steady financing other than UN-assessed contributions, a dearth of training and equipment to achieve genuine interoperability, and the rapid turnover of trained personnel remain perpetual problems for African troop contributors.

European participants endorsed the American consensus on R2P and its appropriate application. They agreed that lack of political will and of international peace enforcement capacity were the most significant factors inhibiting effective international action rather than the constraints of international law.

South Asian participants stressed the importance of state sovereignty and noninterference as key international norms. They viewed UN Security Council authorization as essential to legitimate international intervention and also highlighted the need for Security Council reform to enhance UN legitimacy. South Asian colleagues tended to be skeptical of regional organizations acting without explicit UN blessing, but at least one participant acknowledged the possibility of retroactive UN legitimization if the world deemed the effort to be largely successful, if the intervener made a persuasive legal case for intervention, and if the intervener unconditionally accepted the costs and risks of its action.

Participants from Middle Eastern countries, especially Egyptian representatives, strongly defended national sovereignty. Even though humanitarian interventions may be conducted in the interests of the people of developing countries, they felt it was often the nations of the north exerting their superiority over those of the south. Most Arab interlocutors viewed Iraq as a highly negative precedent, heightening fears that the United States and others will use humanitarian concerns as a pretext for regime change. This perception colored their consideration of any international action in Darfur that does not receive explicit UN support. The Arab League has largely supported Khartoum's efforts to block deployment of an authorized UN force.

Many Mexican participants, for historical reasons, considered state sovereignty as sacrosanct and the principle of noninterference in the domestic affairs of other states as fundamental to their worldview. National law bars Mexican participation in UN peacekeeping operations. Mexican conferees did not agree on whether or not a state's failure to protect its citizens means the international community has a responsibility to do so. However, they all insisted that any such action, particularly involving the use of force, must have explicit UN Security Council authorization.

Finally, Chinese interlocutors accepted the responsibility to protect in concept, as does the People's Republic of China, but interpreted it narrowly in practical terms. Most suggested that there should be high thresholds for international action (for example, that half the population be affected) and that irrefutable evidence of genocide or mass atrocities be gathered and presented by "objective analysts." However, they rejected the UN's findings on Darfur as wrong or biased. One participant suggested that the R2P should only devolve to the international community when a state had collapsed, as in Somalia. Chinese participants placed strong emphasis on the necessity of Security Council backing for any intervention. At the same time, several indicated that the state of U.S.-China bilateral relations and the importance of the target country to Chinese interests might prove more important factors than the R2P when

China considers its reaction to Western-led interventions. In this vein, at least one Chinese participant posited that if a vote were held today, China might be inclined to accept NATO action in Kosovo. Others underscored that China did not object to U.S. intervention in Iraq because the bilateral relationship had improved. Finally, Chinese conferees noted that China rarely has used its Security Council veto (four times) compared to the United States and other council permanent members.

All of the participants recognized that customary international law has evolved since the promulgation of the UN Charter and its insistence on noninterference in the internal affairs of sovereign states. In recent years, they noted, the UN Security Council has defined civil conflicts as threats to international peace and security in such places as Haiti, Cambodia, Bosnia, and Liberia. The Security Council has also given broad latitude to regional organizations under Chapter 8 to act in response to humanitarian and political crises in their respective regions. Participants in our dialogues widely acknowledged that norms have evolved: in the early 1990s the UN acquiesced in the intervention in Liberia by the Economic Community of West African States Monitoring Group (ECOMOG) without a Security Council mandate, and later blessed this mission and subsequent ECOMOG action in Sierra Leone. The Security Council also deferred to NATO in the Balkans, the African Union in Burundi and Darfur, and Australia in East Timor.

The conversations revealed significantly differing approaches to the responsibility to protect. While some experts saw a fully emerged norm that had been wholeheartedly embraced by the international community, others remained deeply committed to the sanctity of national sovereignty. Strong consensus exists, however, that international customary law has evolved, and continues to evolve, on the subject of the responsibility to protect.

Recommendations for International Policy

Our series of regional policy dialogues considered various ideas to strengthen the international normative and practical foundations for humanitarian intervention in the context of massive violations of human rights. The following are proposed recommendations for international policy that draw on the regional dialogues but represent the authors' own views.

EMBRACE ALL THREE ELEMENTS OF R2P

In addition to *reacting* swiftly and effectively to massive violations of human rights, the international community needs to invest far more substantially over the long term in both *conflict prevention* and *postconflict reconstruction*.

Effective prevention requires proactive and coordinated diplomatic engagement at critical stages as the situation grows more fragile. More significantly, it requires efforts to mitigate the root causes of civil conflict—and chief among these may be poverty.[51] A wide body of recent evidence shows that poverty, measured as low GNI per capita, is a significant risk factor for civil conflict. Oxford University professor Paul Collier finds that a country with $250 GDP per capita has a 15 percent risk of falling into civil conflict over a five-year period whereas a country with a GDP of $5,000 faces only a 1 percent risk of conflict over the same period. Good governance and democratic institutions also make critical contributions to conflict prevention by creating and distributing the benefits of economic growth effectively. Members of the Organization for Economic Cooperation and Development, developing countries, and multilateral institutions must commit to robust investments in poverty reduction and democratic institution building to create and sustain positive policy environments in underdeveloped countries.

Effective reconstruction also requires creative and sustained investments in security, democratic institution building, justice, and development. Recent research indicates that such assistance should ramp up gradually (starting with capacity building and technical assistance) and peak at year five of the postconflict period, then continue at high levels for several years. It is crucial that postconflict assistance be funded by assessed UN contributions, as peacekeeping operations are, and not left to ad hoc funding mechanisms or the whims of individual donor governments.

BUILD REGIONAL PEACE OPERATIONS CAPACITY

While some progress has been made in recent years to help developing countries enhance their peacekeeping capacity, much more remains to be done. In particular, the G-8 commitment to train and equip five interoperable subregional brigades in Africa must be fulfilled quickly, and African countries must exercise and sustain these brigades. Regional organizations with capacity limitations should seek assistance promptly and be provided with robust logistical support as well as command, control, communications, and intelligence assistance from external coalitions and partner countries. Regional bodies' decisionmaking processes on whether or not to intervene should not require consensus from all members and should not be subject to veto by a party to the conflict.

STRENGTHEN UN CAPACITY

In 2007 the UN had deployed the second largest ground force in the world, behind only the United States. Although the UN has improved enormously its headquarters capacity over the past fifteen years, key gaps remain, many of which can be blamed on lack of commitment by the UN's most powerful members, including the United States. As of this writing, the UN still lacks any effective rapid deployment capability. Its standby forces initiative exists only on paper. The Permanent Five members, those with the most capable militaries, have all but abandoned UN peacekeeping with the notable exception of China, which has become a major contributor in recent years. Key member states also continue to balk at establishing an effective intelligence–early warning capacity for the UN, which is essential to preventive action. All of these shortcomings should be addressed with utmost urgency under the constructive leadership of the permanent members of the UN Security Council. Finally, the new Peacebuilding Commission has a great distance to travel in order to fulfill its potential.

ESTABLISH LEGITIMATE ALTERNATIVES
WHEN THE SECURITY COUNCIL FAILS TO ACT

At present the international community has no agreed normative framework for halting genocide or massive crimes against humanity when the Security Council fails to do so. This is the case in Darfur where international action has been authorized but not implemented due to lack of resolve to deploy without Sudanese agreement. The following procedures and alternatives should be adopted as the international standard in such instances:

—The Permanent Five members of the UN Security Council should forswear the use of the veto to halt international intervention for humanitarian reasons, unless they publicly articulate a compelling case that their vital national interests are at stake. This is by no means a fail-safe solution since countries can claim that their vital interests are at stake, and no multilateral body has the authority to rule on the validity of those claims. However, it would raise the political bar, help dissipate the constant but ambiguous cloud of a veto threat against humanitarian interventions, open recalcitrant nations to international scrutiny, and increase transparency.

—The UN General Assembly could be convoked in emergency session to vote on "Uniting for Peace" action when the Security Council is deadlocked.

—Decisions to support intervention by relevant or concerned regional bodies should be deemed sufficient to legitimize action by their members when Security Council authorization is sought but not forthcoming.

—When all else fails, a member state or coalition of members may intervene to save lives at their own risk and expense and seek retroactive UN or regional support. In this instance the gravity of the humanitarian crisis, the purity of humanitarian motives, and the efficacy and proportionality of the military action should be critical considerations in the achievement of ex post facto legitimization. Member states that take such action should be prepared to have their intervention formally condemned and penalties assessed if it fails to meet the above criteria. In addition, member states that take such action should be prepared to shoulder the costs of the postintervention responsibilities.

DO NOT FAIL DARFUR AGAIN

The newly established norm of the responsibility to protect will likely die in its crib if the international community fails to act effectively in Darfur. The best hope in this regard is the rapid deployment of a robust Chapter 7 UN force, as authorized by UNSCR 1706. If necessary, this force could be deployed without Sudanese permission. Even with UN advisers and funding, an augmented AU or even UN-AU hybrid force will likely not suffice to save enough civilians and could well prove another cruel hoax to the people of Darfur. The Security Council, acting under Chapter 7, should pass another resolution giving Sudan a very short and finite amount of time to accept the UN force unconditionally or face military consequences by member states, collectively or individually. If the Sudanese do not accept the UN force, the United States should lead an international campaign to enforce the resolution by bombing Sudanese airstrips and military assets, enforcing a no-fly zone over Darfur, and even, perhaps, blockading Port Sudan until Sudan relents. Then UN forces, prepositioned in Chad, could deploy immediately.

If the Security Council fails to respond to the genocide in Darfur, it risks losing, for the foreseeable future, its remaining legitimacy on matters of humanitarian intervention. In the absence of Security Council action, the AU or NATO (an extraregional yet concerned and involved organization) could authorize punitive pressure, as NATO did in Kosovo in 1999. If all else fails, the United States should establish and lead what might be dubbed a "coalition of the compassionate"—and be prepared to accept the consequences.

Conclusion

It was not long ago that the human rights of a victimized population failed even to register public concern, much less initiate government action. The modern forms of human rights protections are a post–Second World War phenomenon. Humanitarian intervention dates back less than twenty years, to the protection of the Kurdish population in northern Iraq after the 1991 Gulf War. It is no small irony that the second Bush administration's surviving rationale for the 2003 invasion of Iraq is the protection of the rights of the Iraqi people under the boot heel of Saddam Hussein. From the low-profile deployment in 1991 to the extraordinarily high-profile pitch for popular support in 2003, human rights concerns have increasingly and vigorously asserted themselves in the public discourse.

As this norm of protecting human lives and human dignity developed in the public mind, officials simultaneously began to regard civil conflict as a threat to international peace. Sovereignty also became an insufficient excuse for maintaining an impenetrable barrier between victims and an effective humanitarian response. Correspondingly, the tools that national governments had to address these concerns matured. Through the crises of Somalia, Haiti, Rwanda, Bosnia, and Kosovo, national leaders learned, their spines stiffened, and they grew accustomed to using all the tools in their toolboxes.

These trends make the failure to respond to current humanitarian disasters even more inexcusable. The outrage and alarm sounded over the continuing genocide in Darfur is a reminder of how far human rights have traveled in the public consciousness in a few short decades. Tragically, it is also a reminder of how far there is to go in translating public concern into effective action. If the emerging norm of the responsibility to protect endangered populations fails to spur a sufficient response in Darfur, then the idea has no more utility than the paper on which it is printed. The instruments exist; sufficient government will, to date, does not. The lives of hundreds of thousands of Sudanese have already been lost; tens of thousands more are in jeopardy. And so is a principle that once bore much promise but requires implementation in real time to make any difference.

Notes

1. Thomas Hobbes, *The Leviathan,* edited by Edwin Curley (1651; reprint, Indianapolis, Ind.: Hackett Publishing, 1994), part 1, chap. 17, p. 106.

2. See United Nations, "Universal Declaration of Human Rights" (www.un.org/Overview/rights.html).

3. Winston Churchill, "Sinews of Peace," speech delivered at Westminster College, Fulton, Missouri, March 5, 1946 (www.winstonchurchill.org/i4a/pages/index.cfm?pageid=429).

4. See American Rhetoric, "John F. Kennedy: Inaugural Address," January 20, 1961 (www.americanrhetoric.com/speeches/jfkinaugural.htm).

5. Anatol Lieven and Will Marshall, "On Might, Ethics and Realism: An Exchange," *National Interest* 86 (2006): 84–91.

6. Stanley Hoffmann, *The Ethics and Politics of Humanitarian Intervention* (University of Notre Dame Press, 1996), p. 16.

7. Francis Fukuyama, *America at the Crossroads* (Yale University Press, 2006), pp. 183–84.

8. Karl Kaiser and Klaus Becher, "Germany and the Iraq Conflict," in *Western Europe and the Gulf,* edited by Nicole Gnesotto and John Roper (Paris: Institute for Security Studies of the WEU, 1992), p. 44.

9. Pierre Lellouche, "Thinking the Unthinkable: Guidelines for a Euro-Defense Concept," in *Europe in the Western Alliance: Towards a European Defense Entity,* edited by Jonathan Alford and Kenneth Hunt (Basingstoke: Macmillan Press, 1988), p. 61.

10. United Nations Security Council, "Resolution 688 (1991)," April 5, 1991 (www.fas.org/news/un/iraq/sres/sres0688.htm).

11. Rajiv Tiwari, "United Nations: Third World Resists Humanitarian Intervention," Inter Press Service, November 6, 1991.

12. Strobe Talbott, "Post-Victory Blues," *Foreign Affairs* 71 (Winter 1991–92): 53–69.

13. David Halberstam, *War in a Time of Peace* (New York: Scribner, 2001), pp. 321–23.

14. "A Quagmire after All," *Newsweek,* April 29, 1991, p. 23, quoted in Samantha Power, *A Problem from Hell* (New York: Basic Books, 2002), p. 241.

15. Francine Friedman, *Bosnia and Herzegovina: A Polity on the Brink* (New York: Routledge, 2004), p. 50.

16. Marvin Kalb, quoting Lawrence Eagleburger, "'The CNN Effect': How 24-Hour News Coverage Affects Government Decisions and Public Opinion," Brookings-Harvard Forum: Press Coverage and the War on Terrorism, January 23, 2002 (www.brook.edu/comm/transcripts/20020123.htm).

17. Brent Scowcroft, quoted in Power, *A Problem from Hell,* p. 293.

18. Ibid.

19. George H.W. Bush, "Text of a Letter to the Speaker of the House and the President Pro Tempore of the Senate," Washington, December 10, 1992 (www.findarticles.com/p/articles/mi_m1584/is_n50_v3/ai_13359713).

20. United Nations Security Council, "Resolution 940 (1994)," July 31, 1994 (lic.law.ufl.edu/~hernandez/IntlLaw/Haiti940.htm).

21. "The Triumph of Evil," *Frontline,* PBS, January 16, 1999.

22. James Traub, *The Best Intentions* (New York: Farrar, Straus and Giroux, 2006), p. 53.

23. Robert Dole, as quoted from *Face the Nation,* CBS, December 11, 1994.

24. *Congressional Record,* June 16, 1994, p. H4559.

25. Anthony Lake, quoted in Power, *A Problem from Hell,* p. 364.

26. Warren Zimmermann, *Origins of a Catastrophe* (New York: Times Books, 1996), p. 7–8.

27. Samuel Huntington, "Clash of Civilizations," *Foreign Affairs* 72 (Summer 1993): 22–49.

28. Robert Kaplan, *Balkan Ghosts: A Journey through History* (New York: St. Martin's Press, 1993).

29. Dick Cheney, interview, *Newsmaker Saturday,* CNN, August 1, 1992, as quoted in Power, *A Problem from Hell,* p. 282.

30. George H.W. Bush, White House briefing, Federal News Service, August 6, 1992.

31. Traub, *The Best Intentions,* p. 42.

32. Sadako Ogata, "International Meeting on Humanitarian Aid for Victims of the Conflict in the Former Yugoslavia," statement of the High Commissioner for Refugees, July 29, 1992 (www.unhcr.org/admin/ADMIN/3ae68fac1a.html).

33. UN Security Council, "Resolution 770," August 13, 1992 (www.ohr.int/other-doc/un-res-bih/pdf/s92r770e.pdf).

34. Lawrence Eagleburger, "Method to the Madness," decision brief (Washington: Center for Security Policy, October 2, 1992), p. 3, as quoted in Power, *A Problem from Hell,* p. 283.

35. See *International Herald Tribune* (Tokyo ed.), March 26, 1998, p. 4; *Croatian Weekly* (Zagreb), July 17, 1998, p. 2, cited in Sabrina Ramet, *Balkan Babel* (Boulder, Colo.: Westview Press, 2002), p. 318.

36. *Frankfurter Allgemeine,* March 16, 1999, p. 1.

37. Karen Donfried, "Kosovo: International Reactions to NATO Air Strikes," in *Kosovo-Serbia: A Just War?* edited by Frank Columbus (Commack, N.Y.: Nova Science Publishers, 1999), p. 103.

38. Quoted in Catherine Guicherd, "International Law and the War in Kosovo," *Survival* 41, no. 2 (1999): 19–34

39. Quoted in Richard McCallister, "French Perceptions," in *Kosovo: Perceptions of War and Its Aftermath,* edited by Mary Buckley and Sally Cummings (New York: Continuum, 2001), p. 94.

40. As quoted by Warren Hoge, "Crisis in the Balkans: Britain; Blair under Domestic Pressure on Ground Forces," *New York Times,* May 18, 1999, p. A10.

41. Quoted in Ivo Daalder and Michael O'Hanlon, *Winning Ugly: NATO's War to Save Kosovo* (Brookings, 2000), p. 127.

42. Independent International Commission on Kosovo, *The Kosovo Report* (New York: Oxford University Press, 2001), p. 4.

43. Ibid., p. 4.

44. Ibid., p. 169.

45. African Union, "Communiqué of the Seventeenth Meeting of the Peace and Security Council," October 20, 2004 (www.africa-union.org/News_Events/ Communiqu%C3%A9s/Communiqu%C3%A9%20_Eng%2020%20oct%2020 04.pdf), p.1.

46. International Commission on Intervention and State Sovereignty, *The Responsibility to Protect,* September 2001 (www.iciss.ca/pdf/Commission-Report.pdf).

47. Ibid., p. xiii.

48. High-Level Panel on Threats, Challenges and Change, *A More Secure World: Our Shared Responsibility* (New York: United Nations, 2004), p. 66.

49. United Nations, *In Larger Freedom: Towards Development, Security and Human Rights for All; Report of the Secretary General,"* March 2005 (www.un.org/largerfreedom/contents.htm).

50. United Nations General Assembly, "2005 World Summit Outcome," October 24, 2005 (unpan1.un.org/intradoc/groups/public/documents/UN/UNPAN 021752.pdf), p. 30.

51. Susan E. Rice, Corinne Graff, and Janet Lewis, "Poverty and Civil War: What Policy Makers Need to Know," Working Paper 2, December 2006 (www. brookings.edu/views/papers/rice/poverty_civilwar.pdf).

CHAPTER FIVE

What the World Thinks

ANNE E. KRAMER

T HE CRUCIAL THREATS to international peace and security—terrorism, the proliferation of weapons of mass destruction, and gross violations of human rights—as described in detail in the preceding chapters, all challenge the rules currently governing the use of force enshrined in the 1945 United Nations Charter. In order to address these challenges, new cooperative strategies must be developed that will meet the twin tests of legitimacy and efficacy. To pass these tests, any set of proposals must not only satisfy U.S. security and foreign policy concerns but also be seen as legitimate and acceptable by the broader international community.

Therefore, the Brookings Institution launched a global dialogue to analyze other nations' perspectives on the legitimate use of military force. Regional discussions over the course of three years focused on when the use of force might be considered—and internationally recognized—as a legitimate response to terrorist threats, the proliferation of weapons of mass destruction (WMD), and humanitarian emergencies. A core group of Americans met with representatives from the major regions, including their counterparts in Europe (France, Germany, the United Kingdom), China, the Middle East (Egypt, Israel, and Iran), Russia, South Asia (India and Pakistan), sub-Saharan Africa (South Africa, Senegal, Democratic Republic of the Congo, Ethiopia, and Kenya), and Latin America (Mexico and Brazil). The participants included a mix of foreign policy scholars, international lawyers, former military officers, and government officials. The interlocutors were only representatives, but their perspectives provide insight into the likely views of their countries on the use of military force to counter international security threats.

This chapter aims to highlight the major areas of agreement on using force to address the primary security challenges of terrorism, WMD proliferation, and humanitarian emergencies. While it is a report of the past three years of dialogues, the views expressed are the author's own interpretations and conclusions. Examination of these perspectives yielded four principal factors as the most important determinates of a state's views on the use of force: threat perception, normative constraints, the efficacy of military action, and legitimacy.

The nature and depth of the threat influences how resolute countries are on the use of military force. The greater and more immediate the perception of the threat, the more willing nations are to act forcefully and the more likely they are to sanction this force at early stages in the deliberations.

Normative considerations shape the context surrounding decisions to use force. As Martha Finnemore argues, norms "shape the rights and duties states believe they have toward one another" along with the goals they value.[1] These norms are primarily behavioral precepts that guide states' actions within the international system. Some norms are strengthened through codification in international law or treaties while others are reinforced through states' continual observance of them. Oftentimes, however, norms are in conflict with one another. The norm of state sovereignty and nonintervention in the internal affairs of other states, harking back to the Treaty of Westphalia in 1648, is one of the more trenchant norms that is slowly beginning to be superseded by the desire to protect innocent citizens from their own governments. States' desire to solve issues peacefully must be balanced against a will to act before greater harm is inflicted. In regard to weapons of mass destruction, some states are more concerned that every country—whether it is Iran, the United States, or Brazil—uphold the near universal nonproliferation norm. Other nations, however, care more if particular countries are complying with the stipulations in the nuclear Non-Proliferation Treaty. When norms come in conflict with one another, how a country balances them—the weight it attributes to one above the other—influences its perspective on when military action is a justified response.

Efficacy relates to whether military action will actually achieve the desired ends. As Richard Haass explains, "The question of whether to use force can never be divorced from the question of how to use it effectively."[2] The efficacy of military action factored prominently in the regional dialogues, with many participants doubting whether force would resolve the fundamental issues at stake.

Legitimacy addresses whether force is viewed as justifiable in a particular instance and who makes this decision. At one end of the legitimacy continuum is a situation in which force is executed in self-defense after an armed attack, which is almost always justified. Such retaliatory attacks include action against a proven threat and uphold a fundamental norm that is codified in the UN Charter under Article 51 as an inherent right of states. At the other end of the legitimacy spectrum lies an act of aggression aimed at territorial conquest, which is regarded as unjustified. Such action clearly violates another codified norm of nonaggression found in Article 2[4] of the UN Charter and represents a threat both to the state acted upon and usually to international security as well. The contentious cases are those that fall in the murky expanse between these extremes. These cases pose critical questions. When is force justified to act against perceived threats, uphold established norms, and effectively resolve a problem? Can one state's belief in the legitimacy of its measures make it so?

Throughout the Brookings discussions, there emerged three main ways force could be legitimized: normative legitimacy (the enforcement of widely accepted norms), substantive legitimacy (the effectiveness of the actual use of force), and procedural legitimacy (the process by which a decision to use force is made). Normative legitimacy centers on upholding the norms referenced above. Whether force is the best way to enforce norms as well as the strength and universality of the norms can determine this type of legitimacy. Substantive legitimacy is based upon the military action's performance in accomplishing its objectives. The efficacy of force obviously plays a large role, and often this is not determined until after the fact. Procedural legitimacy, finally, stems from following steps or going through certain institutions for agreeing upon action. For some Americans, in particular the Bush administration, substantive legitimacy is enough, and nothing justifies military action as much as success. For many non-Americans, however, procedural legitimacy is paramount.

Therefore, the last session of each workshop addressed this crucial issue of who decides. What, if any, type of international or regional institution is capable of legitimizing force? What characteristics must this organization possess in order to grant legitimacy to a military action?

An examination of a nation's views of the aforementioned four determinants, as reflected in the Brookings Institution discussions, highlights where cross-regional consensus lies and where further efforts need to be directed in order to build greater global accord. This chapter analyzes regional perspectives on these factors by looking at the three main security threats addressed in each of the Brookings dialogues.

Terrorism and the Use of Force

Countries basically agree that the use of force is justified either to preempt a terrorist attack or in response to such an attack. The terrorist attacks over the past five years (in New York and Washington on September 11, Bali, Casablanca, Madrid, Riyadh, Beslan, London, Istanbul, and elsewhere) have illustrated the global reach of terrorism and strengthened the resolve that some type of action is necessary. While a global consensus exists for the legitimacy of preemptive attacks against terrorists, the efficacy of force is questioned by some. As it has proved harder than anticipated to root out terrorists in Afghanistan, reservations about using force to deal with terrorism have grown stronger.

THREAT

Terrorism is a shared threat, but there are discrepancies in the depth of this threat. For example, discussions in Russia were held only weeks after the terrorist bombing at the school in Beslan, and consequently, the Russian participants articulated a much more aggressive response than many other interlocutors. Americans share this threat perception—almost 80 percent deem terrorism an extremely important threat.[3] More than eight in ten American foreign policy experts expect another attack on the scale of September 11 within a decade.[4] Europeans believe terrorism endangers national security but to a lesser degree than Americans—66 percent perceive terrorism as an extremely important threat.[5] Conversely, only 42 percent of the Chinese public perceives terrorism as a critical threat.[6] Similarly, South Asian participants in the Brookings discussions argued that the terrorist threat has weakened over the past five years. Their only exception to this lessening threat would be if a terrorist group acquired weapons of mass destruction—a prospect few deemed very likely. Nations that perceive a lower and more distant threat from terrorism have a greater tendency to be cautious about using military force.

While the United States could have approached counterterrorism through more international channels over the past five years, "there were significant substantive differences on the nature of the threat of terrorism that could not have been removed by smoother diplomacy."[7] Put simply, American threat perception was extremely high after September 11, but this deep sense of peril was not shared by much of the international community. While other countries still felt the terrorist threat, it did not dominate their national security agenda to the same extent, contributing to a greater hesitation to employ military force.

While the fear among Americans was especially heightened after September 11, this was not completely unwarranted. Terrorist expert Bruce Hoffman points out that since 1968 the United States has been the number one target of terrorists' attacks worldwide.[8] The position of the United States as the leader of the free world during the cold war and now as the only remaining superpower makes it a particularly attractive target.[9] The pervasive presence of the United States, including the reach of U.S. business overseas and the vast number of diplomatic installations, military posts, and travelers, contributes to this vulnerability. Additionally, the United States has the world's most extensive reach in terms of media, so terrorists know that almost any attack on an American target would receive worldwide attention.

In addition to discrepancies in the depth of the threat, each region confronts a particular terrorist menace—Israel faces Hamas and Hezbollah; Russia, Chechnya; Ethiopia, Somalia; China, the Uighurs. This "my terrorism" problem leads to different definitions of terrorism along with diverse counterterrorism strategies that make it difficult to reach agreement on generic rules for using military force.

NORMS

Basic norms in countering terrorism are less debatable given the nature of the actors and actions. Terrorism by its very definition violates established norms of protecting innocent civilians and stabilizing society. Both the United Nations High-Level Panel on Threats, Challenges and Change and Secretary General Kofi Annan define terrorism as an act "intended to cause death or serious bodily harm to civilians or non-combatants, when the purpose of such act, by its nature or context, is to intimidate a population, or to compel a Government or an international organization to do or to abstain from doing any act."[10] Unfortunately, the UN General Assembly failed to adopt this definition, thus weakening the emergence of a new normative basis for employing force to address terrorism.

The disagreements over the root causes of terrorism that blocked consensus within the UN reflect the national divergences. Many developing nations argued that terrorists could also be defined as occupiers or countries that establish military bases on their land and believed that most definitions were too "Western" to be generally accepted. Also, each region's particular terrorist threat made agreement on one unified definition difficult. As many experts have articulated, one group's "terrorist" is another's "freedom fighter." African participants, while perceiving a real threat from terrorism, found it difficult to agree on concrete norms for defining terrorists since many countries in Africa acquired their independence by employing terrorist tactics. Russian interlocutors raised a similar issue, explaining how Chechens argue that Georgians, Ukrainians, and Estonians gained independence, so they should, too.

After the attacks of September 11, the UN Security Council was able to agree on resolution 1373 reaffirming the right of the United States to act forcefully in self-defense against terrorist activities and de facto legitimizing U.S. military action in Afghanistan. There was very little questioning of the U.S. right to self-defense under Article 51 and NATO's right to act under Article 5 of the NATO treaty. The Taliban regime in Afghanistan was not recognized by the United Nations, so the conflict with state sovereignty that is a decisive factor in most interventions was not a prominent issue. This resolution, as well as the chain of events that secured it, proved exceptional, however. In most situations the norm of nonintervention in the internal affairs of states still clashes with the desire to intervene before innocent civilians are hurt.

EFFICACY

As David Fromkin's seminal article on terrorism argues, "Terrorism achieves its goal not through its acts, but through the response to its acts."[11] Therefore, how can nations respond to attacks in a way that decreases the ability of terrorists to gain even more support? For the most part, sole reliance on military force has been ineffective in stamping out terrorism. Even though the attack on Afghanistan was legitimate and succeeded in rooting out the Taliban and al Qaeda's main base, it has been ineffective in permanently dealing with the threat. However, the U.S. government has continued to place a heavy emphasis on military force as the primary means of countering terrorism. The forceful approach of the United States, illustrated succinctly through the name given to the administration's response—"the war on terrorism"—produced negative reactions even to the concept.[12] As Leslie Gelb argues, "It's clear to nearly all that Bush and his team have had a totally unrealistic view of what they can accomplish with military force and threats of force."[13] Even in Afghanistan, where the United States had a clear objective of removing the Taliban host government and enjoyed the consent of the international community, force alone did not eliminate the threat.

Confronting passive state sponsors of terrorism with primarily military action also yields few results. Instead, as Daniel Byman argues, military strikes are generally counterproductive because they tend to generate increased popular resistance to any cooperation with the attacking nation and reduce incentives for the host government to provide assistance.[14] Both the U.S. air strikes in Libya in 1986 and the launch of cruise missiles against Afghanistan in 1998 increased these countries' determination to support the terrorists while doing little damage to the terrorist organization. Oftentimes, military action against terrorists can serve as the motivation for recruiting new terrorists to undertake further attacks. While almost all participants accepted this dilemma, South Asians and Egyptians voiced this concern most prominently. Due to this conundrum, countries are hesitant to sanction force as a central part of counterterrorism strategies.

Inability to garner international cooperation for implementing military action against terrorists can undermine the efficacy of the action. Throughout the discussions non-American participants continually complained about the lack of intelligence sharing between the United States, other nations, and local authorities. Granted, the United States must be discreet about sharing such information to avoid compromising its vital national interests, and the involvement of too many countries in a counterterrorist operation can encumber action with problems of command and control. Nonetheless, some middle ground needs to be reached. Without quality intelligence, which as the African participants pointed out can often be enhanced by cooperation with local authorities, it is extremely difficult to locate terrorist cells before they attack.

The evolution of the terrorist threat has further highlighted the lack of efficacy in using force. For example, many believe that al Qaeda has transformed from a centralized organization to a loose confederation of individual cells united by a common ideology. Under such circumstances and barring a few obvious exceptions, the threat from terrorists no longer emanates primarily from the states harboring them; thus the kind of military action as was taken against Afghanistan is no longer applicable. This development makes a military approach seem even less efficacious and necessitates a change in counterterrorism strategy. On this basis some Pakistani participants strongly advocated a complete rejection of the use of force to deal with terrorism. Several Egyptians shared this perspective, arguing that "al Qaeda is a state of mind," making it difficult to combat with military tactics.

In adjusting to the transformation of al Qaeda, the international community must also disaggregate the terrorist threat to see which terrorist groups can be most effectively countered with force.[15] U.S. strategy frequently has been too quick to lump most of the terrorist groups together without differentiating between their political aims and the severity of their methods and motives. A practical step, suggested by a South Asian, could be to create a typology of terrorist organizations. Some groups only seek to gain rights and privileges in states, obviously a less drastic goal than that of groups desiring to alter maps. By categorizing terrorist groups, strategists can think in specific terms when deciding on policy. With certain terrorist groups, military action may be the only response capable of resonating with them.

Efforts to implement effective military action often undermine its legitimacy. For example, an attempt to pinpoint and destroy a key military target (such as a terrorist leader or training camp) may lead to significant collateral damage and both local and international criticism. Americans and Egyptians agreed that targeted assassinations were better, particularly ones that largely avoided collateral damage by taking place away from cities. The Israelis pointed out that their response to terrorist actions in the Palestinian conflict is a strategy for their survival. Israel's use of targeted killings is not primarily an attempt to win hearts and minds but rather a response to an immediate threat: if they do not preempt and blow up the bomber, then he or she could kill an entire group of innocent individuals. Targeted killings, Israelis pointed out, are only a preventive measure.

LEGITIMACY

While the efficacy of military action to counter terrorism is questionable in many circumstances, its legitimacy is less in doubt. Participants from across the globe generally concurred that action is legitimate in clear Article 51 situations or cases where force is retaliatory. Since such action falls at one extreme of the legitimacy spectrum discussed above, as well as addresses a clear threat and conforms to agreed norms, its legitimacy is rather clear cut. However, force in self-defense against terrorism may turn out to be ineffective, pointing to an interesting paradox: where force is most legitimate, its efficacy is in gravest doubt.

This contradiction points to the need to establish other norms that could sanction military action early enough to be both effective and legitimate. For the most part, the project interlocutors also supported limited preemptive use of force against terrorist threats. However, defining what constitutes a preemptive attack and who decides that was less clear. The High-Level Panel report defined preemptive force as legal "if the threatened attack is imminent" and "no other means would deflect it."[16] If the threat is less imminent, the action would be preventive, and the panel argued that the Security Council would have to authorize the use of force in that situation.

Those participants from countries that had a lower threat perception of a terrorist attack generally supported this reasoning, which gives greater weight to the norm of nonintervention in the internal affairs of states. As discussed above, the terrorist threat felt by the Chinese is substantially lower than that of Americans, Russians, and Europeans. Thus encroachment on state sovereignty remains their paramount concern. Chinese interlocutors maintained that military action is justified in specific, limited cases of a terrorist training camp or safe house. They set narrow parameters for the use of force to combat terrorism. This policy was evident even in the immediate aftermath of the September 11 attacks. In a phone call with British prime minister Tony Blair on September 18, 2001, then president of the People's Republic of China Jiang Zemin noted that the war on terrorism required conclusive evidence, specific targets, compliance with the UN Charter, and a role for the Security Council.[17]

Arguing that the link between terrorism and the states that harbor them is tenuous and difficult to prove with hard evidence, Chinese participants believed that military action should not be used against a state in most situations. For China, state sovereignty trumps the terrorist threat in all but the most obvious and imminent cases.

On the other hand, nations having a strong threat perception of terrorist attacks did not support the absolute necessity for the UN Security Council to grant legitimacy, even when the threat was latent. American and Russian participants pointed out that their threats from terrorism were often more imminent than others in the Security Council. Similarly, Ethiopians pointed to the pressing threat they felt from Somalia but doubted other organizations, especially regional ones, would agree to sanction force. Left with these differences, there was no agreement reached on the preventive use of force for countering terrorism—that is, in instances when the threat is not deemed imminent by the UN.

These situations point to the fundamental question: how many states must agree that a threat is imminent in order to warrant military action? Many participants believed agreement among regional organizations was necessary to at least represent a quorum. However, if this is not possible, is the targeted state justified in forcefully dealing with the threat alone? Or if agreement is not forthcoming, does this imply that the targeted state has an inflated perception of the threat? Conference participants generally agreed in theory that international consensus was preferable. But when participants faced their own national terrorist situations, they were not ready to write off the notion of determining what constituted self-defense. Ultimately, if a state's national security interests are endangered, it will not submit to other countries' approval. Thus the United Nations risks becoming irrelevant if it cannot authorize some type of response in these instances, and individual states will then turn to other means.

For situations where the validity of using force falls more into a gray area, the three aforementioned avenues to legitimacy—substantive, normative, and procedural—have yet to be backed by international consensus. There have been limited occasions when force has proved effective in combating terrorism, so testing substantive legitimacy is challenging. The United States and its allies were able to root out the Taliban base from Afghanistan, but this was already a retaliatory attack. For many participants, the lack of past examples as clear successes indicated that substantive legitimacy was not a viable justification for using force against terrorism. In addition, by its nature substantive legitimacy is retroactive, and thus it does not help in providing legitimacy at the beginning of an operation. Furthermore, the lack of international approval at the outset can contribute to terrorist recruitment, making legitimacy granted after the fact even less useful.

Normative legitimacy ran into difficulty with the conferees due to the conflicting norms of nonintervention in the internal affairs of states and the desire to act before greater harm is done. The differences in threat perception and the resulting divergent emphases on corresponding norms make agreement on this approach problematic. However, future consensus in this area may be possible due to the increase in Security Council resolutions on combating terrorism. In particular, Indian participants pointed to such Security Council resolutions over the past five years as an important means of establishing norms for international action to combat terrorism.[18]

Procedural legitimacy did hold some weight. Most participants accepted the legitimacy of action if regional organizations or the UN were able to agree that a threat required a forceful response. Differences of opinion primarily arose over whether the UN Security Council was the exclusive authorizer or just the preferred authorizer. Many times this division occurred more between international lawyers and military strategists than along national lines. With the heavy focus on the limited efficacy of force throughout conference discussions, Americans pointed out that doing nothing is an inadequate response for combating terrorism. Instead, efforts need to focus on how to reduce the disutility of force. If military action is the result of multilateral institutions that have the ability to rally the necessary communities, then force is viewed as more legitimate, and this reduces the ability of terrorists to galvanize additional support. Consequently, the answer is to develop mechanisms to isolate the terrorists and make the action a response not only from the target but also from the larger community. For example, if an Islamic group were to condemn a specific terrorist attack that was in support of a radical Islamic fundamentalist agenda and then support a retaliatory response, including the potential use of military force, the further rallying cry of terrorists would be undermined. If the leaders who carry credibility with the community support action, it becomes harder for terrorists to claim they are battling the "evil" United States. While such cooperation may be a way off, efforts could focus more on how to work with multilateral structures to increase its likelihood.

To achieve such cooperation, it is crucial to frame actions to combat terrorism as part of a global effort. One Pakistani offered a telling example of a nongovernmental organization trying to educate the *madrassa* teachers on international law. The NGO changed the teachers' perspective dramatically by illustrating the different documents approved by the United Nations that articulated a global call to fight terrorism and explaining these antiterrorist efforts as part of Pakistan's strategic responsibilities to the international system.[19] If individuals can gain greater appreciation that antiterrorism actions are part of a global endeavor, then these efforts are no longer about fulfilling obligations to the United States. Instead, they can be viewed as Pakistan upholding its commitments as a crucial component in combating terrorism worldwide.

These types of exercises work toward changing the perception of terrorism from a narrow, national threat to a collective security challenge. Such an evolution will take time, but as terrorists continue to threaten societies across the globe, it may become more of a reality. Working on codifying norms through international institutions such as the United Nations can only help in coalescing international agreement for more effective actions to combat terrorism. While military action should remain only one facet of a larger counterterrorism strategy, discussions emphasized that greater global cooperation is needed in order to make the sometimes necessary application of force legitimate.

Weapons of Mass Destruction and the Use of Force

As with terrorism, weapons of mass destruction pose a shared threat, but assessments diverge over the nature and depth of the threat. Nations perceive this threat differently and consequently focus on the corresponding distinct norms—either compliance or nonproliferation. Both of these norms are eroding, making international consensus based on them extremely difficult. The efficacy of using military action to enforce nonproliferation is even more debatable, both because of the difficulty in destroying a nation's WMD program and the U.S. debacle in Iraq. The combination of clear threats, a discriminatory norm, and the questionable effectiveness of force highlights the need for new rules.

THREAT

Countries agree that the proliferation of WMD poses a threat, but they differ on the primary concern. On the whole most states are troubled by the erosion of the near universal nonproliferation norm, believing that violations, regardless of the nation, will embolden and enable future actors to proliferate. From this perspective the particular state attempting to acquire nuclear weapons and its past actions are not the central threat; rather it is the larger challenge presented to the nonproliferation regime. European interlocutors along with Egyptians and Mexicans tended toward this perception. They focused on the general state of noncompliance with the Non-Proliferation Treaty (NPT), which makes it difficult to sanction force against one offender while other violators have not faced similar consequences. For instance, consideration of military action against Iran for its attempts to enrich uranium should be tempered since the international community would probably not endorse similar action against Brazil for its comparable efforts. This universalistic perspective leads to a collective security rationale, labeling proliferation a threat to international peace and security and thus subject to military action under Chapter 7. Consequently, international agreement to sanction force is an even higher priority.

On the other hand, some countries subscribe to a particularistic threat assessment, believing that it is the nature and intentions of the individual country possessing or attempting to possess WMD capabilities that determine the threat. Force is justified if the threat from the state is sufficiently grave—which depends in part on the particular state's past actions. Participants from the United States, Israel, and, surprisingly, China were more emphatic that the threat stemmed primarily from the nature of the state rather than from the acquisition of a particular technology. To China such a threat would exist if Taiwan or Japan were to acquire nuclear weapons but not North Korea—though Chinese participants recognize the U.S. concern. Chinese interlocutors articulated that since the threat is specific to each nation, proliferation should be considered a matter of traditional national security, where a state's actions to deal with the threat would fall into the self-defense category.

Given China's decidedly realist perspective regarding proliferation, it would support forceful action if the threat were severe. Indeed, the Chinese participants argued that preemptive use of force designed to prevent a state that clearly has aggressive intent from acquiring nuclear weapons could be justified as a form of anticipatory self-defense (that is, under Article 51 of the UN Charter). The key to such use of force would be clear evidence that the threatening state in fact had acquired a WMD capability. For example, Chinese participants agreed with American participants that the 1998 bombing of Iraq, when Saddam expelled the International Atomic Energy Agency inspectors, was justified. They even suggested that a similar campaign in 2003—as opposed to the full-scale war that actually ensued—would likely have garnered Beijing's support.

Differences also extend to the degree that proliferation is perceived as a challenge to a country's national security. Israeli and American participants maintained a deeper threat perception than others. Israelis believe that Iran represents an existential threat, not least because of Iranian president Mahmoud Ahmadinejad's threats to "wipe Israel off the map." Americans share a pressing threat perception—seven out of ten Americans believe that the possibility of unfriendly nations becoming nuclear powers represents a critical threat to U.S. vital interests.[20] Yet only three out of ten Chinese citizens view this as a threat.[21] Other countries fall somewhere between, with a majority of Europeans believing the threat from Iran is real but not as pressing and urgent a matter as most Americans.[22]

Because their perception of threat was less than that of Americans, many participants from other nations would state that the proliferation of WMD was "unacceptable," but they oftentimes did not reach the point of sanctioning military action to prevent such conditions from materializing. With a lower threat perception, these countries reluctantly acquiesced to living with seemingly intolerable situations rather than employing force except in the most extreme cases.

NORMS

The difference between universalistic and particularistic threat perception points to competing norms in addressing the issue: the nonproliferation norm and the compliance norm. Those states that hold a universalistic perspective place greater weight on the nonproliferation norm, believing that all countries should abide by the stipulations of the NPT, whether that country is the United States, Brazil, or Iran. On the other hand, countries with a particularistic threat perception emphasize the compliance norm, focusing on specific nations that are not abiding by the NPT.

The difficulty with the compliance norm is reaching agreement within the broader international community on the particular states that should follow the NPT. If it depends on the state's threat to another nation, it will be difficult to reach a global consensus. To build an effective regime, it is easier to point to clear norms that are being violated as opposed to deciding on a case-by-case basis which violation constitutes a real threat. However, because the NPT has declared that only some states are legally allowed to possess nuclear weapons to ensure their security, the nonproliferation norm based upon it is discriminatory and ineffective, providing a weak basis for legitimizing military action.

Those participants focusing on the nonproliferation norm stressed how North Korea suffered few consequences when it withdrew from the NPT, so using force against Iran for its NPT violations would be furthering the discrimination in the enforcement of the treaty. In addition, Israel, Pakistan, and India failed to uphold the general nonproliferation norm and suffered no military consequences. In fact, many believe that the recent U.S.-India civilian nuclear deal undermined the NPT bargain by providing India with nuclear material—the major incentive to join the NPT—without requiring it to relinquish its nuclear weapons capability or to sign onto the NPT. With these challengers of the NPT not suffering military consequences, it becomes harder to view the use of force as a justified response to similar proliferation threats in the future.

Non-nuclear states, along with non-NPT signatories but declared nuclear powers, argued that the central bargain in the NPT is undermined by the failure of the nuclear powers to abide by Article 6 of the NPT—to negotiate the disarmament of their nuclear capabilities. Even though Article 6 is conditional on behavior with regard to the second pillar of the treaty (states not seeking nuclear weapons), U.S. development of more advanced nuclear weapons, Russia's emphasis on the centrality of its nuclear forces to its new defense posture, Britain's decision to modernize its deterrent, and the continuous modernization of nuclear weapons by France and China all undermine the arguments by these nuclear powers that they are complying with the spirit, if not the letter, of their NPT commitment.

The NPT is also ineffective because it allows states to pursue a nuclear program for peaceful purposes, which they can also use concurrently as a basis for developing a nuclear weapons program. For example, even farmers in Iran invoke the NPT as granting their country the authority to develop nuclear energy for peaceful purposes.[23] However, that same authority provides Tehran with an inherent capability to build nuclear weapons.

Participants strongly agreed upon the need to establish a broader norm for nonproliferation. While there are certain steps that can be taken, it will take time to develop any meaningful treaty, and if the 2005 NPT Review Conference is the forecast of things to come, resolution of the necessary issues will be difficult, if not impossible. Some participants, such as the Egyptians, approached the NPT like the UN Security Council—deeply flawed but the best game in town. Some interlocutors from non-nuclear-weapon states stressed the need for disarmament as the principal way forward.

Other participants emphasized the emergence of new norms. For example, interdiction under the Proliferation Security Initiative is gaining broader acceptance. The Proliferation Security Initiative, a U.S.-led coalition structured to improve enforcement of laws against shipping nuclear, biological, and chemical weapons–related materials, was constructed from already existing national and international laws. It has been successful in expanding its membership due to its voluntary nature, enforcement of existing laws, and near universal desire to halt trans-shipments.[24] While it specifically sanctions interdiction of vessels carrying such material, also implied in the initiative's plan is use of military force if ships do not cooperate.[25] The success of this norm illustrates the way forward for the international community to strengthen efforts to stem proliferation of WMD.

Another promising area of consensus coalesced around the threat of nuclear terrorism that necessitated clear action. The five NPT and three undeclared nuclear weapons states (India, Pakistan, and Israel) agreed that passing nuclear material to terrorists or nonstate actors should be deemed illegal, with the transferring state being held accountable. Pakistanis, and even some Indians, did not go as far as Americans in believing that this included states transferring nuclear weapons capabilities to other states accused of sponsoring terrorism. Another idea gaining widespread endorsement was to build on UN Security Council Resolution 1540, which establishes measures to limit the acquisition of WMD by nonstate actors, as the normative basis for opposing proliferation of any kind.

EFFICACY

Once again the efficacy of military action was a significant factor in deter-mining its legitimacy. It is extremely hard, if not impossible, to completely destroy a state's capability to build nuclear weapons. One may be able to devastate a facility but not an entire national program. Instead, the best that can be hoped for is to delay the nuclear program. Also, it is impossi-ble to destroy the technical and scientific knowledge and infrastructure, which will allow a state to rebuild after an attack with even greater fer-vor. In addition to the enormous political costs of a preemptive strike against a nuclear program in peacetime, there is a risk of a counterstrike, which could even include a surrogate terrorist attack or the retaliatory targeting of economic infrastructure.[26]

Examples from history illustrate the efficacy, or lack thereof, of mili-tary attacks. The Israeli bombing of Iraq's Osirak reactor in 1981 suc-ceeded in delaying Iraq's nuclear program. This setback proved crucial since Iraq, as a result, did not have nuclear weapons when it invaded Kuwait in 1990. An Iraq equipped with nuclear weapons might have deterred the allies' counterattack, or Saddam Hussein might have unleashed such weapons against the Kuwaitis. Immediately after the attack, the UN Security Council, including the United States, condemned Israel's tactics. However, Israel's actions now are viewed as relatively legitimate. When inspectors entered Iraq only nine years later, Iraq's nuclear weapons program proved far more advanced than most had anticipated. Thus surgical strikes can sometimes delay action, but ulti-mately the attacked country is able to rebound.

While a surgical strike might now be viewed as legitimate, the tactics of the adversary have evolved, as have international views about such an action. A clear drawback of military attacks is that states developing nuclear weapons adapt to account for the possibility of future strikes. Now it is much more difficult than in the Osirak case to decapitate a nuclear program. Iraq went underground afterward as did, to a certain extent, both North Korea and Iran. Although the attackers' capabilities have improved, so have the adversaries' nuclear programs: instead of building nuclear reactors, now there are numerous centrifuges; instead of one main facility, there are many; instead of aboveground facilities, now they are underground. These changes make a surgical strike, for instance against Iran, an uncertain prospect.

Indeed, a surgical strike was not even an option with North Korea in 1994. The radiation fallout, along with possibly instigating a war with South Korea, would have made a strike counterproductive. General Gary Luck, commander of U.S. forces in South Korea at the time, even stated, "If we pull an Osirak, they will be coming south."[27] The effectiveness of the alternative U.S. strategy of coercive diplomacy is less clear. U.S. secretary of defense William Perry's threats and redeployments of U.S. forces to the theater against North Korea may have affected Pyongyang's decision to freeze its plutonium production program, but that is hard to know at this point. North Korea did sign on to the 1994 U.S.–North Korean Agreed Framework, and it kept its fuel rods in a cooling pond and did not remove them until after the second Bush administration renounced the agreement.[28]

Of course, the ultimate example of a preventive strike against WMD is the 2003 invasion of Iraq, which dominated debates among the participants. To most the Iraq war illustrates the failures of intelligence and makes a clear case against unilateral use of force. Even though intervention makes sense from a theoretical standpoint, carrying out such a policy can be counterproductive and increase instability in the region. Furthermore, the Iraq war raises the issue of whether regime change is necessary to ensure that proliferation is not a threat. Many in the U.S. government, focusing on the particularistic threat, believed that the fundamental character of the regime must be changed. Regime change became a polarizing issue throughout discussions as most non-Americans believed such an extension of the nonproliferation policy was unjustified.

LEGITIMACY

Given the questionable efficacy of a preemptive strike along with the discriminatory nature of the nonproliferation regime and differing levels of threat perception, reaching international consensus on the legitimacy of a preventive or preemptive strike is extremely difficult. Preventive force is regarded as that which is taken before the threat is deemed imminent. Consequently, by its very definition, preventive action allows enough time for further steps to be taken before the application of military force. On the other hand, preemptive force is viewed as action against an imminent threat—one with clear intentions and the capability to execute an attack. However, in the age of nuclear terrorism, the difference between prevention and preemption is increasingly blurred. Instead, a country's possession of nuclear material and the possibility of it supplying terrorists or other nonstate actors with such material make preventive force a serious option. Once a country has the capacity to make and deliver weapons of mass destruction, whether the threat is imminent or not can be a matter of minutes. If the use of preemptive force is only considered legitimate when a country's WMD program has developed enough to qualify as an imminent threat, then force may be too late to be effective—the material may already have been transferred or be ready for deployment. This point underscores the efficacy-legitimacy paradox discussed earlier: force is most effectively used early in the development of a gathering threat but is least likely to be supported at that point, whereas by the time support for using force might actually exist, its effectiveness will be more doubtful.

Faced with this efficacy conundrum as well as more robust security threats, some American and Israeli participants argued that preventive action can be regarded as self-defense and thus does not require a Security Council resolution. Other countries contended that a nation usually has an alternative to force, and thus such action cannot be defined as self-defense. The latter tend to agree with the High-Level Panel that if a threat is real but not imminent, there is time to go to the Security Council because the alternative of unilateral action would be tantamount to anarchy: "allowing one to so act is to allow all."[29]

If a state feels strongly that it faces an imminent threat, but the Security Council does not agree, there is the slight possibility that substantive legitimacy will be granted after the fact. Israel's strike against Osirak and the ex post facto legitimacy some countries bestowed upon the act may hold lessons for today. Although it was viewed as illegitimate at first, it accomplished its goal, thus lessening the political fallout. A key factor for Israel in launching the Osirak attack was first gaining public legitimacy through three years of diplomatic efforts. In conference discussions Israelis defined five conditions necessary for using military force: an existential threat is posed, response is time sensitive (reactors will go critical), behavior in acquiring nuclear weapons is well documented and not based solely on national intelligence, all other alternatives are exhausted, and international norms are clearly violated. While agreeing on these conditions, other participants believed that if a situation clearly meets these standards, the Security Council should decide on military action. Thus, while a state may receive legitimacy after the fact, approval by the UN Security Council is still more desirable.

But is the Security Council the deciding factor in such cases, or can a state, or group of states, decide upon a particular action? For providing unquestionable procedural legitimacy to the use of force, UN Security Council approval is still the gold standard. If the UN Security Council concurs that a Chapter 7 threat to international peace and security is involved, military action would be justified. But if member nations do not reach the tipping point to endorse preventive action, who decides when force would be legitimate? Most countries have rejected unilateral wars of regime change to counter proliferation. Given that the Brookings discussions occurred as the situation in Iraq deteriorated, most participants were extremely hesitant to approve the use of force outside of the United Nations. Despite arguments by some Americans that the Iraq war was sanctioned by preceding resolutions, most participants believed that the inability to obtain the final UN resolution authorizing force was a valid reason why the United States should not have invaded Iraq. Throughout conference discussions, Europeans were careful not to state that force could be used in any particular case without UN approval, for fear of setting a dangerous precedent.

The viewpoints on legitimacy diverged even more widely between participants from the West and the Islamic world. As one Iranian pointed out, the Islamic world will regard further use of military force in the Middle East region as an illegitimate U.S. attempt at regime change. The current Bush administration's actions in Iraq serve to confirm the perception of most Middle Easterners that the United States seeks nonproliferation through regime change. Indeed, the U.S. administration's consistent assertion that it will counter proliferation by using force against threatening governments reinforces this belief. Focusing primarily on regime change to alter a nation's nuclear policy undermines political assurances. Instead, a country that sees its survival in jeopardy is further motivated to acquire nuclear weapons for deterrence.

As an alternative, new norms that are stronger and more universally enforced need to be developed. If such standards can be implemented, the possibility for normative legitimacy of military force is greater. For new rules to be accepted, there must be trade-offs between the nuclear haves and have-nots. If the international community wants to avoid the proliferation of nuclear technologies, even the nuclear powers will need to accept certain limitations. Most obvious is working toward negotiating the Fissile Material Cutoff Treaty and ratifying the Comprehensive Test

Ban Treaty. Another possibility, further down the road, is an internationalization of the nuclear fuel cycle.

In general, agreement for using force preventively to counter nuclear proliferation is still very elusive. Normative constraints with greater universal appeal that are seen as enforcing international standards fairly may prove helpful in granting legitimacy. However, first there must be greater consensus among nations of the importance of both the nonproliferation norm and the compliance norm. As former secretary of state Henry Kissinger argues, "A realistic policy will bring a resolution to this debate and emphasize that a wise strategy will recognize the threat inherent in the very fact of proliferation, which can be mitigated but not ended by the existence of benevolent government."[30] Coalescence around the preeminence of the collective threat will be needed to enable more concrete action to be taken by the international community.

Humanitarian Intervention and the Use of Force

Humanitarian interventions authorized by the UN Security Council elicited general approval among the discussion participants, with differences emerging mainly in the stipulations placed on it. Agreement in favor of humanitarian intervention stems from shared threats, emerging norms, and a belief that military action, if given the proper resources, can address the immediate humanitarian emergency. A relative consensus on these issues, along with the moral justification of addressing grave abuses of human rights, provides greater legitimacy for military action. However, the sometimes unintended consequence of regime change can taint the genuine humanitarian nature of certain engagements and thus highlight global differences over military action. In tandem with the Brookings discussions, international deliberations over the crisis in Darfur have provided a sobering example as to where a theoretical consensus in favor of greater humanitarian action stands in practice. The UN failure to adequately address this humanitarian crisis points to the weakness of international support for the use of force unless consensus on its legitimacy is apparent.

THREATS

Whether a humanitarian emergency affects an individual country directly or indirectly, there is a growing consensus that widespread humanitarian abuses can pose a threat to international peace and security. The ability to reach a Chapter 7 agreement on such issues illustrates the universal nature of such threats. Indeed, in the past two decades, the UN Security Council has recognized humanitarian crises as threats to international peace and security in Somalia, Iraq in 1991, Haiti, Bosnia, and Liberia.

For the most part, countries agree that states lacking a capacity to meet the basic human rights of their citizens can be a threat to the region by easily spreading conflict or by deteriorating into failed states. Consequently, they can become high risks to the international community by generating large refugee flows, serving as a breeding ground for terrorism, or, more generally, creating conditions such as extreme poverty and unemployment that are conducive to further conflict.

States that view themselves as global actors with global responsibilities are more sensitive to such threats. The United States and major European countries have already voiced this concern. The 2002 U.S. National Security Strategy argued, "America is now threatened less by conquering states than we are by failing ones."[31] Similarly, the 2003 European Security Strategy explained how the majority of state conflicts over the past decade have been within rather than between states, adding, "State failure is an alarming phenomenon, that undermines global governance, and adds to regional instability."[32] Consequently, the major powers have reached greater consensus on the right—and need—to act forcefully to deal with these situations.

Surprisingly, China's emerging role as a great power resulted in a shift of its strategic interests, moving it toward greater accord with the other global powers. This phenomenon, along with China's growing presence across the world—including $6.6 billion in investments in Africa alone— has resulted in more realistic views of what is in China's interests in the international community.[33] Consequently, Chinese interlocutors expressed greater support for humanitarian intervention, albeit with significant thresholds.

There is still somewhat of a divide between the United States and Europe and countries of the Middle East, Latin America, and South Asia, which perceive threats stemming from outside intervention in a state's internal affairs. As discussed earlier, intervention is more difficult after the 2003 war in Iraq because there is a greater tendency, especially in the Middle East, to view force as part of a larger agenda for regime change. Given the Bush administration's explanation that humanitarian concerns factored into its decision to use force in Iraq, some Middle Eastern participants perceive grave humanitarian abuses as unfounded justification for Western intervention. Moreover, due to the greater regional instability the Iraq war has produced, Middle Eastern nations are skeptical that military force will alleviate human suffering.

Given the negative history of foreign intervention in Mexico, Mexican participants were hesitant to establish a clear precedent for military action on humanitarian grounds for fear that the United States would use it as justification for intervention in Latin America. Mexican interlocutors expressed adherence to their historical perception that threats to their nation are more likely to arise from the United States than from gross violations of human rights.

NORMS

Norms of state sovereignty and nonintervention in the internal affairs of states are in conflict with newly evolving principles of conditional sovereignty and the "responsibility to protect" that call for external intervention. Under the doctrine of responsibility to protect, sovereign states have a responsibility to protect their own citizens from "avoidable catastrophe—mass murder and rape, ethnic cleansing by forcible expulsion and terror, and deliberative starvation and exposure to disease"; but if a state is unwilling or unable to do so, responsibility falls to the international community.[34] This principle was first articulated by the International Commission on Intervention and State Sovereignty in 2001 and was approved by both the UN High-Level Panel and the secretary general in his report, *In Larger Freedom*.[35] In 2005 the UN World Summit "recognize[d] our shared responsibility to take collective action, in a timely and decisive manner, through the Security Council should peaceful means be inadequate and national authorities be unwilling or unable to protect their populations."[36]

For the most part, conference participants supported the norm of the responsibility to protect, agreeing that military action would be legitimate to end grave abuses of human rights. However, there remain regional differences on the notion of conditional sovereignty. These emerged in the stipulations placed on military action that prohibit actual implementation of the responsibility to protect norm. A Security Council resolution with a forceful mandate, invoking Chapter 7, is the ideal that would clearly override the principle of nonintervention. Given the difficulty in reaching this type of consensus, the presence of the emerging norm of the responsibility to protect at least makes it easier for states to point to a clear violation of an agreed standard that would warrant a forceful response.

Discussants from countries that perceived threats as originating from internal state conflicts placed less emphasis on authorization of the Security Council for military action and were more accepting of the concept of conditional sovereignty. Europeans, Americans, and Africans agreed on the importance of building up the responsibility to protect doctrine and intervening forcefully to stop egregious human rights violations. If the Security Council did not authorize action to respond to a state's failure to protect its citizens, these countries would support regional or other multinational organizations undertaking action themselves. Europeans and Americans drew upon the precedent of Kosovo in 1999. Anticipating a Russian veto of military force to stop Serbian attacks on ethnic Albanians in Kosovo, the United States and its allies obtained authorization for action from NATO instead. While it was technically illegal, the intervention afterward proved legitimate in the eyes of the international community.

Africans strongly supported the responsibility to protect doctrine, believing that commitment to it could prevent widespread human suffering on the continent. The African perspective on intervention has evolved significantly. In the earlier postcolonial period, the norm of nonintervention in African countries was stronger. But human security issues and events over the past couple of decades—from Rwanda to Liberia and Sierra Leone—have painfully illustrated the dangers of focusing solely on state sovereignty. Instead, Africans made a significant choice in crafting the new African Union (AU) to specifically endorse the responsibility to protect norm in its founding charter—the only multilateral organization to do so. Now Africans have come to view nonintervention as a greater threat to their lives than external intervention.

Chinese perceptions of conditional sovereignty have also evolved from their original adherence to strict state sovereignty and narrow interpretation of Article 2[4] of the UN Charter. One Chinese participant even posited that China now would have viewed action in Kosovo more positively, given the greater trust between China, Europe, and the United States as well as a clearer understanding of the situation. However, the stipulations that they place on intervention reveal their guarded view of the responsibility to protect norm—most likely for fear of its future application in Tibet, Xinjiang, Taiwan, and other non-Han areas of the country. Thus Chinese interlocutors placed a premium on Security Council involvement in all stages—from an assessment that human rights violations were severe enough to warrant action to approval and, finally, to controlling any resulting operation. The Chinese did not believe that delegating such responsibility to a regional or multinational organization would hold much credibility. Clear thresholds, such as genocide or cases where more than half the population were affected, had to be crossed before action could be warranted. One Chinese participant even maintained that external action would only be warranted in cases where the state had already collapsed, such that there would be no violation of state sovereignty if there were an outside intervention.

Russians and Middle Eastern participants expressed similar doubts over claims of grave human rights abuses, pointing to the instances of regime change that Western states have brought about after justifying intervention on humanitarian grounds. In order to override state sovereignty, a situation required an unbiased assessment clearly illustrating severe violations. This issue has arisen throughout Security Council discussions on Darfur, where China, Russia, and Qatar have voiced skepticism on whether the violations found by the UN investigation team were accurate or grave enough to warrant outside intervention.

Mexican participants disagreed strongly with almost any state intervention, believing that the sovereignty of nations was paramount. Mexican law prohibits intervention in the internal affairs of other countries, harking back to the country's history of external intervention from the United States. Thus this nonintervention principle, which has yet to evolve to the next level as it has with African nations, dominated the deliberations. Mexicans believed that their law would prohibit endorsing military action for gross violations of human rights. They were particularly worried that the responsibility to protect principle might extend to matters dealing with drug trafficking or organized crime. On the other hand, interlocutors from other Latin American countries where citizens' lives had been threatened by a dictator's gross human rights violations, such as Chileans under the dictator Augusto Pinochet, believed intervention could be justified.

EFFICACY

Military capacity to change the situation on the ground and effectively alleviate the suffering of innocent civilians plays a significant role in garnering international consensus for forceful humanitarian intervention. The efficacy of force can be evaluated with three interrelated objectives: addressing the immediate humanitarian emergencies—halting the genocide, providing food—while foreign military troops are present; resolving the humanitarian grievances for the long term, so that the killings do not resume immediately after troops are withdrawn; and establishing a sustainable peace. International discussions highlighted both the importance but also the immense challenge of achieving all three goals. Addressing just the imminent humanitarian crisis is far easier, but such a narrow focus is usually too short sighted to prevent the reemergence of the crisis once troops leave. For example, in Bosnia, NATO was successful in stopping the killings, but ten years later, there is still no lasting framework for political and economic stability. And Iraq has illustrated the extreme difficulty in postconflict reconstruction, even with the United States pouring vast economic and military resources into the country over the past four years. The current capacity of the international community to create a viable, long-lasting peace and tangibly improve the situation on the ground in the long term is not yet adequate.

Although capacity has improved over the past decade, most countries are not willing to provide the troops and equipment necessary to carry out missions. UN peacekeeping operations are increasingly staffed primarily by developing countries—mainly India, Bangladesh, and Pakistan—that may lack the military skills and equipment necessary to get the job done. Regional organizations have tried to fill this gap, but they suffer similar problems with low troop levels, insufficient logistical support, and poor equipment. This problem exists across the board, albeit to different degrees, from the African Union in Darfur to NATO in Afghanistan.

The capacity dilemma is further exacerbated if outside intervention facilitates a regime or state collapse. This sometimes unintended effect makes states more hesitant to sanction military action. In addition to the political consequences, such upheaval can result in greater instability for the region, thus undermining the very reasons for the initial intervention: to alleviate the suffering of innocent civilians. It was just such concern about regional instability that hindered consensus on intervention among the discussants. This perspective was particularly evident among Middle Eastern participants. South Asians were divided in evaluating the capacity of international troops to carry out such endeavors. Africans, while stressing the lack of capacity, believed that with the necessary logistical and military assistance, the African Union could become a viable regional organization for performing humanitarian tasks.

American participants stressed the responsibility to rebuild after intervention, to provide some type of future political and economic framework for the country after the violence has subsided. The responsibility to protect doctrine adopted by the UN General Assembly primarily emphasizes one component—the responsibility to react—while omitting the other important aspects of the three-part doctrine first articulated by the International Commission on Intervention and State Sovereignty: the responsibility to rebuild and responsibility to prevent. Indeed, participants concurred that all three of these aspects are necessary in order to truly protect people.

Unfortunately, the capacity to rebuild after military intervention is even lower than that for initial action. The UN's largest peacekeeping operation, in the Democratic Republic of the Congo, has shown how thinly stretched the UN is for peacekeeping troops and capacity. The new UN Peacebuilding Commission is intended to facilitate reconstruction and stabilization in postconflict countries, but the verdict is still out on whether this body will have the resources, both economically and politically, to implement its own recommendations.

LEGITIMACY

In determining the legitimacy of intervention for humanitarian emergencies, the issue of who decides again proved contentious. All participants agreed that if the Security Council sanctioned military action, it would be deemed legitimate. However, experience has shown that the thresholds that must be crossed in order to garner such agreement ultimately decrease the effectiveness of military intervention: the situation on the ground must be so dire for consensus to be reached that many innocent civilians will have already died. Thus the inverse relationship between efficacy and legitimacy that has applied to countering WMD proliferation and terrorism also applies to humanitarian emergencies.

Indeed, participants from countries that did not endorse the responsibility to protect doctrine as strongly also favored an extremely high threshold to legitimize military action. This stance, articulated by some Chinese, South Asian, and Russian conference participants, makes timely *preventive* action impossible and excludes interventions for all but the most extraordinary violations of human rights. While such stipulations will restrict interventions that have ulterior motives or do not appropriately assess the necessary resources, advocating too far in this direction curtails military action that could be effective in preventing atrocities. Another aspect of the responsibility to protect doctrine—the responsibility to prevent large-scale crisis—should be given greater emphasis. In principle, all participants agreed that more energy and resources should be invested in preventing events from reaching the level that necessitates military force.

Frustrated that UN action is often too late to be effective, Americans, Europeans, and Africans agreed that regional organizations could decide to intervene if the UN were unwilling or unable—even if this meant acting while the state's government was still in power. If military action had the capacity to assuage the problem, the threat from such grave human rights abuses was severe enough to warrant military intervention to uphold the responsibility to protect. Participants from these nations maintained that particularly if the operation proved successful, there would be substantive legitimacy granted to the use of force. The different evaluations of the military force used in Kosovo versus Iraq vividly illustrate the importance of performance in determining the legitimacy of a humanitarian intervention.

The intervention in Kosovo violated the procedure for just and legitimate military intervention because there was no Security Council resolution explicitly authorizing force. However, events afterward contributed to its legitimacy ex post facto. First, it proved an effective response to an imminent humanitarian catastrophe. In addition, the UN authorized an operation in Kosovo after NATO's initial intervention, conferring legitimacy on the original decision. Third, a Russian resolution in the UN Security Council condemning NATO's action failed by a vote of thirteen to two. Last, an independent international commission deemed it legitimate after the fact. Consequently, the Kosovo intervention is now regarded by many as a legitimate military act by NATO. However, South Asian and Russian participants in the Brookings discussions opposed this viewpoint. Therefore, for most—but not all—countries, substantive legitimacy, combined with some type of procedural components, can help establish the legitimacy of an intervention retroactively.

In contrast, the 2003 invasion of Iraq provides an example of how events after the fact can erode legitimacy. At the beginning of the U.S. attack in March 2003, some scholars argued that it could still be deemed legitimate—but not legal—ex post facto. However, the United States did not find concrete evidence of a threatening WMD program, nor was it able to establish stability. In fact, many believe that the U.S. military action in Iraq has created greater instability not only in the country but in the region as well. This unsatisfactory outcome has thus undermined the potential for retroactive legitimacy to be conferred on the Iraq war.

If a country employs force without following international procedures, then legitimacy is possible if the operation proves successful. However, that country will be judged harshly if matters are made worse.

Situations that would warrant military intervention and be likely to confer ex post facto legitimacy are primarily those where established laws are clearly violated. South Asian participants articulated four conditions under which retroactive legitimation would be possible. An international body must determine that there are clear violations of international humanitarian law (using the standards defined by the Rome Statute of the International Criminal Court on genocide, crimes against humanity, and war crimes), violations of human rights (the exact threshold for this is still controversial), violations of the right to self-determination, or threats to foreign nationals.[37] If the situation in a country meets one of these criteria, then it will be easier to receive international support for the use of force to implement an already agreed-upon treaty or other normative principles.

Procedural legitimacy can be hard to attain due to the long process and high thresholds for intervention maintained by members of the Security Council. On the other hand, substantive legitimacy can be tenuous at best since events afterwards can heavily influence the international perspective. Thus normative legitimacy could be a possible future avenue to focus on if the emerging norm of the responsibility to protect takes root. To implement this norm and act even when it is the central government perpetrating the crimes will require an acceptance that sovereignty is conditioned on whether a state provides basic human rights to its citizens. Such a monumental change in the international system will take time, as the situation in Darfur vividly illustrates.

THEORY INTO PRACTICE

UN Security Council resolution 1706, which authorizes deployment of a UN mission of at least 20,600 troops and police to Darfur, invokes for the first time the responsibility to protect doctrine and allows force under a Chapter 7 mandate.[38] However, it still requires the consent of the Khartoum government—a condition that reflects the international refusal to override national sovereignty, even in a situation many view as a prima facie case. In addition, China and Russia, as well as Qatar, abstained from resolution 1706, a response that challenges their support of the responsibility to protect norm and exemplifies how economic interests can trump humanitarian concerns. The Chinese representative at the UN argued that the UN's findings in Darfur were wrong and biased, an assertion congruent with the comments of some of the Chinese and Russian conference participants, who questioned how to verify that grave human rights violations had occurred. China and Russia also abstained from earlier resolutions on Darfur, and fear of China's veto has prevented a strong resolution mandating economic sanctions against Sudan.

However, there are several hints that China may be very slowly altering its stance. At a November 2006 UN-AU emergency meeting on Darfur, the Chinese government persuaded the Khartoum government to finally allow a hybrid UN-AU force into Darfur.[39] With its robust economic presence in Africa, China may be starting to view its role in Africa with a broader perspective. As the Chinese representative to the UN explained with respect to the latest Darfur agreement, "It has good intentions, so therefore I think that we have to work creatively, not to put a strait jacket on ourselves by our former positions."[40] Whether this shift in position will extend beyond Africa to places where China's national interest is not potentially threatened is highly questionable, but as scholar Edward Luck argues, "Africa is a bellwether for Chinese attitudes on intervention."[41]

The efficacy of force is further complicating agreement over military intervention. Susan Rice, Anthony Lake, and Donald Payne argue that military action, specifically enforcement of a no-fly zone and a naval blockade of Sudan's oil ports, is necessary to force the Khartoum government to agree to international resolutions.[42] On the other hand, Stephen Morrison and Chester Crocker believe that such forceful action would be counterproductive to efforts to negotiate with the government.[43] Even the cochair of the commission that first articulated the responsibility to protect doctrine, Gareth Evans, believes military action against the wishes of the Khartoum government could result in greater instability.[44] Furthermore, if the government were to collapse, neither the United States nor the United Nations has the political will or capacity to occupy another Islamic country, especially since the Sudanese government, which has lent significant help to the United States in fighting al Qaeda in the region, has threatened to welcome global jihad.

Darfur's location in an already unstable region further aggravates the problem. Sudan has only recently come under a tenuous north-south agreement ending twenty years of civil war. There is a civil conflict in neighboring Central African Republic, and Darfur refugees and rebels are infiltrating Chad. International powers worry that with further upheaval there will not be enough troops to stabilize the region. However, this context makes some type of intervention all the more necessary since the violence can spread further if it is not checked in Darfur.

The lack of troops to contribute to the mission does make calls for action difficult. UN member countries have not lived up to their responsibility to supply the 20,600 troops that the Security Council was finally able to authorize. The AU has reached its capacity, NATO is stretched thin with commitments in Afghanistan, and the United States is bogged down in Iraq.

Humanitarian intervention is gaining legitimacy in terms of established norms. However, the questions of capacity and efficacy not only make implementation of established doctrines difficult but also can affect their legitimacy after the fact. If states can begin to address the capacity issue, there might be greater willingness to enforce a norm that is gradually taking root. If not, a nascent concept might collapse in a matter of several years.

International and Regional Organizations

As described earlier, resolutions passed by the UN Security Council provide clear legitimacy for military action. This view was shared by all conference participants. Applying agreed rules through an established process produces a broad, widely accepted preference to go to the Security Council first to authorize military action. There is a procedural legitimacy granted to military action that is sanctioned by the council. This consensus reveals an interesting paradox: states are pushing for a greater UN role in legitimating military action despite a growing conviction that the Security Council's credibility, legitimacy, and effectiveness are declining. While the UN does need to be reformed, it is still indispensable for achieving broad-based support for the use of force.

A key reason for international support of the Security Council is the belief by many that it can or will restrain the United States. As Richard Falk points out, in a unipolar world, "international law assumes a more important role than within global settings where countervailing centers of state power exist, providing the only available source of constraining discipline for the United States."[45] The rise of the United States to a position of primacy has increased the restraining role of other institutions since states alone do not necessarily have that ability. The 2003 invasion of Iraq by a U.S.-led coalition illustrated the inability of the UN to prevent American action. However, the difficulty that the United States now faces in Iraq, the inability to find WMD, along with the U.S. attempts to pass a further UN resolution for action, illustrates the value and almost necessity of Security Council approval.

Given this need for the UN, its reform is vital. Participants agreed that the Security Council should be altered but reached no consensus on the specifics. Expectedly, there was a divide between the conferees from the five countries with permanent membership on the council (United States, United Kingdom, France, China, and Russia) and those from other nations regarding expansion of the Security Council. The Chinese interlocutors, who cherish their country's veto power and status in the Security Council, were hesitant to support any reform that reduced China's standing. Other participants from the permanent member countries argued that the challenges of decisionmaking and ineffectiveness would only worsen with additional members on the council. Participants from nonpermanent member countries all voiced a desire for greater representation but as a group did not agree on a central plan for restructuring the composition of the council. South Asians were the strongest advocates for enlarging the Security Council, arguing that it was losing credibility by its lack of representation. However, despite this drawback of limited representation, most interlocutors still concurred that the UN is the best source of legitimacy.

In addition to Security Council reform, some have articulated the need for different rules to govern the body. The High-Level Panel report argued that "the task is not to find alternatives to the Security Council but to make it work better than it has."[46] In order to enhance the Security Council's effectiveness within its current structure, several participants supported the idea of an informal meeting twice a year between the permanent five members and the secretary general to discuss major issues and problems. Alongside this summit there would be a separate meeting with all heads of state of the current membership of the Security Council.

Other participants, including Americans, also argued for the need for additional rules to govern the Security Council, such as stipulations on how the permanent five countries use their veto power. Under this provision, if a country is going to use its veto, it must illustrate and publicly defend how the veto is central to that country's security interests. If the state cannot supply an adequate defense, then it should not be allowed to cast its veto. While other conference interlocutors believed that this was an already understood and generally accepted practice within the Security Council, some argued that it should become a specific statute signed by the members.

While these various ideas might increase the effectiveness of the Security Council, the problem remains as to what steps can be taken when the council fails to act. Secretary General Kofi Annan even pointed out that "unless [the United Nations] is able to assert itself collectively where the cause is just and the means available, its credibility in the eyes of the world may well suffer" and other means will need to be explored.[47] However, the High-Level Panel and the secretary general failed to answer the critical question of what recourse states have when the UN proves unable or unwilling to act. Throughout the Brookings discussions, the role of regional organizations was emphasized as a possible alternative. Even though the UN was created to address only the actions that states and regional organizations could not take (codified in Article 53), there has since been a shift to viewing UN approval as paramount and then resorting to regional organizations if the UN does not act.

Regional organizations provide a compromise on legitimate action since they are predefined coalitions that authorize action. Ideally, the regional organization most immediately affected by the threat would act. Members of regional organizations are more likely to share similar assessments of the threat and also may be more willing to cooperate in responding to it in a timely manner. Such organizations may also have more resources—or at least be better able to command such resources from their members—than global institutions. For these reasons the conference participants, in concurrence with the High-Level Panel, stressed the important role regional organizations should play in dealing with threats to peace and security. There is the possibility, articulated in the High-Level Panel report, that regional organizations may seek Security Council authorization after the operation. This idea of ex post facto authorization has been practicable in the past, and its use may increase with an augmented role for regional organizations.

Each regional organization is structured differently, encumbered by its own set of problems and difficulties. Most organizations are not as established as NATO, which already has a mandate to administer resolutions and the military capacity to carry these out. Other regional organizations would have to undertake difficult legal procedures to make enforcement doable. Among the conferees Africans expressed the most comprehensive and enthusiastic support for regional organizations. The African Union is evolving but suffers from capacity and funding issues—similar to, but greater than, NATO's early struggles. The AU has advanced quickly, but it still has a long road ahead before it is an effective organization that can adequately address regional security militarily. Efforts by the United States and EU to build AU capability may increase its capacity.[48]

With the lack of strong regional organizations in East Asia or strong bilateral ties, China maintains a stronger attachment to the UN Security Council in order to remain a prominent player in multilateral organizations. Recognizing that the reality is changing, Chinese participants were interested in exploring how regional organizations might become more active in the distant future—perhaps initially focused on addressing common challenges such as international crime and terrorism. The Asian security organizations (the Association of Southeast Asian Nations [ASEAN], ASEAN Regional Forum, and Asia Pacific Economic Cooperation) are slowly evolving, but they are not yet at the level of dealing with greater security issues. Their rule by consensus often prohibits actions; one participant even suggested that regional organizations should be governed by majority rule rather than universal consensus in order to allow action. Interestingly, the Organization for Security and Cooperation in Europe has a consensus-minus-one principle which enabled it to act against human rights violators in Yugoslavia. Application of this principle to other regional organizations may assist in ending stalemates and allow greater progress in decisionmaking.

Israelis also argued that the regional approach carries the greatest legitimacy aside from the Security Council, but they face the problem in the Middle East of having no regional organization that encompasses everyone. Egyptians were less enthusiastic about the role of regional organizations, believing that they would only be able to produce minimal benefits.

The Mexican participants, who clearly come from a more formal rule-based and institution-based perspective on these issues, did not see an inherent problem with using regional organizations, but they deemed it unlikely that the United States would address crucial security concerns through the Organization of America States (OAS). However, the OAS has proved important in the past. For example, in 1994 it was important to have OAS consensus for the intervention in Haiti so that the action was not interpreted as a dominant America enforcing its will unilaterally in Latin America.

Even though both the UN and regional organizations have their problems, conference participants concurred that coalitions of the willing were not the answer. The lack of organization before the mission severely hurts the legitimacy granted by the international community. Several Americans articulated the need for a concert of democracies as a way to counter this. A concert of democracies, as articulated in the introduction by Ivo Daalder, would be made of a group of like-minded states that could sanction military action early enough for it to be effective but also have greater legitimacy.[49]

Conclusion

One of the most interesting, albeit disappointing, findings was the inverse relationship between legitimacy and efficacy. This paradox led the Brookings group to arrive at an interesting matrix, depicted in figure 5-1. The use of force matrix relates the efficacy of using force and its legitimacy under different circumstances. In the top right corner, the case of interstate conflict, the defensive use of military force enjoys both a high degree of legitimacy and, depending on the balance of forces, a high degree of efficacy. In the top left corner, instances of retaliatory military action against a terrorist attack possess the greatest legitimacy but suffer from a lack of efficacy. At the bottom left corner, use of force to confront proliferation of weapons of mass destruction is likely to be both less effective and enjoy less legitimacy. Finally, humanitarian intervention (which straddles the top and bottom right corners) exemplifies a situation where force can be used with a comparatively high degree of efficacy and is increasingly likely to be considered legitimate.

The aim of policy is to develop processes and capabilities that can move each of these interventions into the top right corner—where the use of force is both legitimate and effective. The problem is the apparent trade-off between legitimacy and military effectiveness. In an age of

Figure 5-1. Use of Force Matrix: Legitimacy versus Efficacy

		Low	High
Legitimacy	High	Counterterrorism	Self-defense
			Humanitarian intervention
	Low	Counterproliferation	
		Low	**High**

Efficacy

nuclear terrorism and genocide, early, preemptive, if not preventive, uses of force are likely to prove most effective but are also considered least legitimate. At a later stage, responsive military action is likely to be more legitimate but also less effective. The need is to develop cooperative strategies that will provide a meaningful alternative to unilateralism or institutional paralysis and be both legitimate and effective.

Part of building these strategies is strengthening the main determinates—emphasizing shared threats, establishing stronger norms, employing force where it has a greater likelihood of being effective, and doing so through multilateral means that will also provide greater legitimacy. Granted, countries will always have their unique threat perceptions, but a greater appreciation for the challenges that are at the forefront for other countries may facilitate reciprocal understanding. For example, much of the developing world is threatened first and foremost by HIV-AIDS and other pandemics. Not only will assistance from the West on these issues produce greater goodwill between the nations, it may also mitigate the cascading effect in donor countries. In an increasingly globalized and interconnected world, such threats know no borders.

Greater appreciation of each other's critical threats will hopefully enable the development of solid norms that correspond to meeting these challenges. The greater the clarity of the norms and the more unified states are in upholding them, the more likely they are to serve as constraints as well as an appropriate trigger for the use of force when necessary. The Proliferation Security Initiative with its codification of norms is an example that has already demonstrated some success. Using such efforts as a template may be a promising way to establish consensus in other areas.

The most important norm that is evolving and slowly gaining international support is the concept of conditional—as opposed to absolute—state sovereignty. Greater acceptance of this norm will require considerable time and effort, but the increasing likelihood of global threats originating locally necessitates its adoption. Thus, if a state sponsors terrorism, develops weapons of mass destruction, or grossly violates human rights, it "forfeits the normal benefits of sovereignty."[50] Promulgating the view of sovereignty as a responsibility rather than a right entails codifying the principles of state conduct.[51] Clear normative standards will minimize discrimination in the process of determining whether a state is no longer fulfilling its obligations and the use of force is necessary.

The efficacy of force should be demonstrable if countries are to take the additional step of sanctioning its use. There is no one-size-fits-all solution for improving the effectiveness of military action in addressing the different threats this project has examined. For humanitarian intervention there is a clear need for increased capability to carry out robust operations. With terrorist threats and WMD proliferation, the answer is less clear cut, but both require greater international consensus. A global response and commitment to counter terrorist threats can reduce the ability of terrorists to rally further support the way they can from a unilateral use of force. In countering the proliferation of WMD, the threat of force is a more credible deterrent if states show greater unity on the need to act.

Development in all three of these areas—appreciation of collective threats, establishment of stronger norms, and effective military action—will increase the legitimacy of the use of force. Then military action can be seen as a constructive way to enforce norms that address security threats. If such foundations exist, it may prove easier to pass action through international institutions. While the UN Security Council will remain the preferred authorizer for the near future, regional organizations or other multilateral structures could acquire greater ability to legitimize action, or at least greatly encourage the UN to act by being a competitive entity. Legitimacy would then be attainable through a mix of normative, procedural, and substantive criteria. Granted, this is a goal that is still a long way off, but if small steps are taken in each of these areas, there will be some hope for greater global consensus on the use of force.

Notes

1. Martha Finnemore, *The Purpose of Intervention* (Cornell University Press, 2003), p. 53.

2. Richard Haass, *Intervention* (Brookings, 1999), p. 68.

3. German Marshall Fund and others, *Transatlantic Trends: Key Findings 2006* (www.transatlantictrends.org/trends/doc/2006_TT_Key%20Findings%20 FINAL.pdf), p. 7.

4. This statistic on this question remained unchanged over the past two surveys undertaken by the Center for American Progress and the journal *Foreign Policy*. See "The Terrorism Index," July-August 2006 (web0.foreignpolicy.com/ issue_julyaug_2006/TI-index/index.html), and February 2007 (www.american progress.org/issues/2007/02/pdf/terrorism_index.pdf).

5. German Marshall Fund, *Transatlantic Trends: Key Findings 2006*, p. 7.

6. Chicago Council on Global Affairs, *The United States and the Rise of China and India: Results of a 2006 Multination Survey of Public Opinion* (2006), p. 35.

7. Richard A. Falk, "Legality and Legitimacy: The Quest for Principled Flexibility and Restraint," *Review of International Studies* 3, suppl. S1 (December 2005): 33–50.

8. See Bruce Hoffman, *Inside Terrorism* (Columbia University Press, 2006), pp. 178, 341. Comprehensive data on terrorist attacks from 1968 to present are found in the RAND Terrorism Incident Database. The one exception to the United States as the prime target was in 1997, which witnessed an unusually high number of Kurdish and Turkish terrorist attacks on each other in Germany.

9. Ibid.

10. High-Level Panel on Threats, Challenges and Change, *A More Secure World: Our Shared Responsibility* (New York: United Nations 2004), p. 52. See also United Nations, *In Larger Freedom: Towards Development, Security and Human Rights for All; Report of the Secretary General* (New York, 2005), p. 35.

11. David Fromkin, "The Strategy of Terrorism," *Foreign Affairs* 53, no. 4 (1975): 683–98.

12. Gilles Andreani, "War on Terrorism: Wrong Concept," *Survival* 46, no. 4 (2004): 31–50.

13. Quoted in "The Terrorism Index," July-August 2006.

14. Daniel Byman, "Confronting State Sponsors of Terrorism," Analysis Paper 4 (Washington: Saban Center for Middle East Policy, February 2005), p. 3.

15. Audrey Kurth Cronin, "How al-Qaida Ends: The Decline and Demise of Terrorist Groups," *International Security* 31, no. 1 (2006): 7–48.

16. High-Level Panel, *A More Secure World,* p. 63.

17. Shirley A. Kan, "U.S.-China Counter-Terrorism Cooperation: Issues for U.S. Policy," Report RS21995 (Congressional Research Service, Library of Congress, May 12, 2005), p. 2.

18. UN Security Council resolutions on terrorism include 1373, which offers an international package of measures to curb terrorism; 1624, which calls on states to prevent the incitement of terrorism; and 1540, which limits the acquisition of WMD by terrorists.

19. These documents included the UN Charter and the UN Security Council resolutions on terrorism cited above.

20. Chicago Council on Global Affairs, *United States and the Rise of China and India,* p. 64.

21. Ibid., p. 35.

22. According to one poll, 75 percent of Americans versus 58 percent of Europeans believe Iran represents an extremely important threat. German Marshall Fund, *Transatlantic Trends: Key Findings 2006,* p. 7. See also Charles D. Ferguson and Peter van Ham, "Beyond the NRA Doctrine," *National Interest* 87 (January-February 2007): 55–60.

23. In discussing his documentary on Iran, Ted Koppel detailed his conversation on nuclear bombs with a small landowner twenty miles outside of Isfahan. Koppel explained, "We start talking about the bomb, and even in Farsi I can hear he's saying 'NPT,' non-proliferation treaty. He's invoking the non-proliferation treaty and saying, 'We have a right. Why can't we, you know, the Pakistanis have it, and the Israelis have it and the Indians have it. Why shouldn't we have it?'" Ted Koppel, *Meet the Press,* November 19, 2006 (www.msnbc.msn.com/id/15751399/page/5/).

24. Peter Dombrowski and Rodger A. Payne, "The Emerging Consensus for Preventive War," *Survival* 48, no. 2 (2006): 115–36.

25. Ibid., p. 124.

26. Bennett Ramberg, "Preemption Paradox," *Bulletin of Atomic Scientists* 62, no. 4 (2006): 48–56.

27. Ibid.

28. Larry A. Niksch, "North Korea's Nuclear Weapons Development and Diplomacy," Report RL33590 (Congressional Research Service, Library of Congress, January 3, 2007), p. 16.

29. High-Level Panel, *A More Secure World,* p. 63.

30. Henry A. Kissinger, "The Rules on Preventive Force," *Washington Post,* April 9, 2006, B7.

31. White House, *The National Security Strategy of the United States of America* (September 2002), p. 1.

32. "A Secure Europe in a Better World: European Security Strategy," Brussels,

December 12, 2003 (www.consilium.europa.eu/uedocs/cmsUpload/78367.pdf), pp. 2, 5.

33. According to the Chinese Ministry of Commerce, China had invested $6.64 billion in forty-nine African countries by the end of 2006. "Value of Sino-African Trade Reaches $50 Billion in 2006," Asia Pulse News Service, February 1, 2007.

34. International Commission on Intervention and State Sovereignty, *The Responsibility to Protect,* September 2001 (www.iciss.ca/pdf/Commission-Report.pdf).

35. High-Level Panel, *A More Secure World,* pp. 64–65. See also United Nations, *In Larger Freedom.*

36. UN General Assembly, "2005 World Summit Outcomes," A/60/L.1 (September 20, 2005), p. 31.

37. For more information on the Rome Statute, see United Nations, "Rome Statute of the International Criminal Court," July 1998 (www.un.org/law/icc/statute/romefra.htm).

38. Military force is only allowed to protect threatened civilians, UN personnel, and humanitarian workers in operations that support the implementation of the Darfur Peace Agreement. The team would include 17,300 military personnel, 3,300 civilian police, and up to sixteen Formed Police Units. Consent is only "invited" to this deployment, not formally required, but troop-contributing countries are presently unwilling to take part in any deployment to which Khartoum does not agree. International Crisis Group, "Getting the UN into Darfur," Africa Briefing 143, October 12, 2006 (www.crisisgroup.org/home/index.cfm?id=4442&l=1).

39. U.S. special envoy to Sudan Andrew Natsios praised Chinese UN ambassador Wang Guangya for gaining Khartoum's cooperation, stating, "At critical moments, he intervened in a very helpful and useful way." Colum Lynch, "China Filling Void Left by West in UN Peacekeeping," *Washington Post,* November 24, 2006, A12.

40. Wang Guangya, quoted in Evelyn Leopold, "UN Official Blames Sudan for Worsening Darfur Crisis," Reuters, November 22, 2006.

41. Quoted in Lynch, "China Filling Void."

42. Susan E. Rice, Anthony Lake, and Donald Payne, "We Saved Europeans, Why Not Africans?" *Washington Post,* October 2, 2006, p. A19.

43. J. Stephen Morrison and Chester Crocker, "Time to Focus on the Real Choices," November 7, 2006 (www.washingtonpost.com/wp-dyn/content/article/2006/11/06/AR2006110600813.html).

44. Gareth Evans, "A Rule-Based International Order: Illusory or Achievable?" Rustow Memorial Lecture, City University of New York, September 19, 2006.

45. Falk, "Legality and Legitimacy."

46. High-Level Panel, *A More Secure World,* p. 65.

47. Kofi Annan, "Two Concepts of Sovereignty," *Economist,* September 16, 1999.

48. The Bush administration's five-year, $660 million Global Peace Operations Initiative, was launched in 2004 to train and equip 75,000 peacekeepers, a majority of them African. Similarly, in April 2004 the EU established the €250 million African Peace Facility to support African-run peacekeeping operations in Africa and strengthen the capacity of the AU to design, plan, and implement peace operations. See Nina M. Serafino, "The Global Peace Operations Initiative: Background and Issues for Congress," Report RL32773 (Congressional Research Service, Library of Congress, February 16, 2005), p. 1; and International Institute of Strategic Studies, *Strategic Survey 2004–2005* (London: 2005), p. 231.

49. Ivo Daalder and James Lindsay, "Democracies of the World, Unite," *American Interest* 1, no. 2 (2007): 5–15. See also G. John Ikenberry and Anne-Marie Slaughter, *Forging a World under Law and Liberty: U.S. National Security in the 21st Century,* September 2006 (www.wws.princeton.edu/ppns/report/FinalReport.pdf), pp. 25–26, 61.

50. Richard Haass, "Sovereignty," *Foreign Policy* (September-October 2005): 54.

51. Ibid.

Excerpts from

The Responsibility to Protect:
Report of the International Commission
on Intervention and State Sovereignty (2001)

Synopsis

THE RESPONSIBILITY TO PROTECT: CORE PRINCIPLES

(1) Basic Principles

A. State sovereignty implies responsibility, and the primary responsibility for the protection of its people lies with the state itself.

B. Where a population is suffering serious harm, as a result of internal war, insurgency, repression or state failure, and the state in question is unwilling or unable to halt or avert it, the principle of non-intervention yields to the international responsibility to protect.

(2) Foundations

The foundations of the responsibility to protect, as a guiding principle for the international community of states, lie in:

A. obligations inherent in the concept of sovereignty;

B. the responsibility of the Security Council, under Article 24 of the UN Charter, for the maintenance of international peace and security;

C. specific legal obligations under human rights and human protection declarations, covenants and treaties, international humanitarian law and national law;

D. the developing practice of states, regional organizations and the Security Council itself.

(3) Elements

The responsibility to protect embraces three specific responsibilities:

A. **The responsibility to prevent:** to address both the root causes and direct causes of internal conflict and other man-made crises putting populations at risk.

B. **The responsibility to react:** to respond to situations of compelling human need with appropriate measures, which may include coercive measures like sanctions and international prosecution, and in extreme cases military intervention.

C. **The responsibility to rebuild:** to provide, particularly after a military intervention, full assistance with recovery, reconstruction and reconciliation, addressing the causes of the harm the intervention was designed to halt or avert.

(4) Priorities

A. **Prevention is the single most important dimension of the responsibility to protect:** prevention options should always be exhausted before intervention is contemplated, and more commitment and resources must be devoted to it.

B. The exercise of the responsibility to both prevent and react should always involve less intrusive and coercive measures being considered before more coercive and intrusive ones are applied.

THE RESPONSIBILITY TO PROTECT: PRINCIPLES FOR MILITARY INTERVENTION

(1) The Just Cause Threshold

Military intervention for human protection purposes is an exceptional and extraordinary measure. To be warranted, there must be serious and irreparable harm occurring to human beings, or imminently likely to occur, of the following kind:

A. **large scale loss of life,** actual or apprehended, with genocidal intent or not, which is the product either of deliberate state action, or state neglect or inability to act, or a failed state situation; or

B. large scale 'ethnic cleansing,' actual or apprehended, whether carried out by killing, forced expulsion, acts of terror or rape.

(2) The Precautionary Principles

A. **Right intention:** The primary purpose of the intervention, whatever other motives intervening states may have, must be to halt or avert human suffering. Right intention is better assured with multilateral operations, clearly supported by regional opinion and the victims concerned.

B. **Last resort:** Military intervention can only be justified when every non-military option for the prevention or peaceful resolution of the crisis has been explored, with reasonable grounds for believing lesser measures would not have succeeded.

C. **Proportional means:** The scale, duration and intensity of the planned military intervention should be the minimum necessary to secure the defined human protection objective.

D. **Reasonable prospects:** There must be a reasonable chance of success in halting or averting the suffering which has justified the intervention, with the consequences of action not likely to be worse than the consequences of inaction.

(3) Right Authority

A. There is no better or more appropriate body than the United Nations Security Council to authorize military intervention for human protection purposes. The task is not to find alternatives to the Security Council as a source of authority, but to make the Security Council work better than it has.

B. Security Council authorization should in all cases be sought prior to any military intervention action being carried out. Those calling for an intervention should formally request such authorization, or have the Council raise the matter on its own initiative, or have the Secretary-General raise it under Article 99 of the UN Charter.

C. The Security Council should deal promptly with any request for authority to intervene where there are allegations of large scale loss of human life or ethnic cleansing. It should in this context seek adequate verification of facts or conditions on the ground that might support a military intervention.

D. The Permanent Five members of the Security Council should agree not to apply their veto power, in matters where their vital state interests are not involved, to obstruct the passage of resolutions authorizing military intervention for human protection purposes for which there is otherwise majority support.

E. If the Security Council rejects a proposal or fails to deal with it in a reasonable time, alternative options are:
  I. consideration of the matter by the General Assembly in Emergency Special Session under the "Uniting for Peace" procedure; and
  II. action within area of jurisdiction by regional or sub-regional organizations under Chapter VIII of the Charter, subject to their seeking subsequent authorization from the Security Council.

F. The Security Council should take into account in all its deliberations that, if it fails to discharge its responsibility to protect in conscience-shocking situations crying out for action, concerned states may not rule out other means to meet the gravity and urgency of that situation—and that the stature and credibility of the United Nations may suffer thereby.

(4) Operational Principles

A. Clear objectives; clear and unambiguous mandate at all times; and resources to match.

B. Common military approach among involved partners; unity of command; clear and unequivocal communications and chain of command.

C. Acceptance of limitations, incrementalism and gradualism in the application of force, the objective being protection of a population, not defeat of a state.

D. Rules of engagement which fit the operational concept; are precise; reflect the principle of proportionality; and involve total adherence to international humanitarian law.

E. Acceptance that force protection cannot become the principal objective.

F. Maximum possible coordination with humanitarian organizations.

(. . .)

2. A New Approach: "The Responsibility to Protect"

2.1 Millions of human beings remain at the mercy of civil wars, insurgencies, state repression and state collapse. This is a stark and undeniable reality, and it is at the heart of all the issues with which this Commission has been wrestling. What is at stake here is not making the world safe for big powers, or trampling over the sovereign rights of small ones, but delivering practical protection for ordinary people, at risk of their lives, because their states are unwilling [or] unable to protect them.

2.2 But all this is easier said than done. There have been as many failures as successes, perhaps more, in the international protective record in recent years. There are continuing fears about a "right to intervene" being formally acknowledged. If intervention for human protection purposes is to be accepted, including the possibility of military action, it remains imperative that the international community develop consistent, credible and enforceable standards to guide state and intergovernmental practice. The experience and aftermath of Somalia, Rwanda, Srebrenica and Kosovo, as well as interventions and non-interventions in a number of other places, have provided a clear indication that the tools, devices and thinking of international relations need now to be comprehensively reassessed, in order to meet the foreseeable needs of the 21st century.

2.3 Any new approach to intervention on human protection grounds needs to meet at least four basic objectives:

—to establish clearer rules, procedures and criteria for determining whether, when and how to intervene;

—to establish the legitimacy of military intervention when necessary and after all other approaches have failed;

—to ensure that military intervention, when it occurs, is carried out only for the purposes proposed, is effective, and is undertaken with proper concern to minimize the human costs and institutional damage that will result; and

—to help eliminate, where possible, the causes of conflict while enhancing the prospects for durable and sustainable peace.

2.4 In the later chapters of this report we spell out in detail how these objectives might be met. But there is a significant preliminary issue which must first be addressed. It is important that language—and the concepts which lie behind particular choices of words—do not become a barrier to dealing with the real issues involved. Just as the Commission found that the expression "humanitarian intervention" did not help to carry the debate forward, so too do we believe that the language of past debates arguing for or against a "right to intervene" by one state on the territory of another state is outdated and unhelpful. We prefer to talk not of a "right to intervene" but of a "responsibility to protect."

2.5 Changing the language of the debate, while it can remove a barrier to effective action, does not, of course, change the substantive issues which have to be addressed. There still remain to be argued all the moral, legal, political and operational questions—about need, authority, will and capacity respectively—which have themselves been so difficult and divisive. But if people are prepared to look at all these issues from the new perspective that we propose, it may just make finding agreed answers that much easier.

2.6 In the remainder of this chapter we seek to make a principled, as well as a practical and political, case for conceptualizing the intervention issue in terms of a responsibility to protect. The building blocks of the argument are first, the principles inherent in the concept of sovereignty; and secondly, the impact of emerging principles of human rights and human security, and changing state and intergovernmental practice.

THE MEANING OF SOVEREIGNTY

The Norm of Non-Intervention

2.7 Sovereignty has come to signify, in the Westphalian concept, the legal identity of a state in international law. It is a concept which provides order, stability and predictability in international relations since sovereign states are regarded as equal, regardless of comparative size or wealth. The principle of sovereign equality of states is enshrined in Article 2.1 of the UN Charter. Internally, sovereignty signifies the capacity to make authoritative decisions with regard to the people and resources within the territory of the state. Generally, however, the authority of the state is not regarded as absolute, but constrained and regulated internally by constitutional power sharing arrangements.

2.8 A condition of any one state's sovereignty is a corresponding obligation to respect every other state's sovereignty: the norm of non-intervention is enshrined in Article 2.7 of the UN Charter. A sovereign state is empowered in international law to exercise exclusive and total jurisdiction within its territorial borders. Other states have the corresponding duty not to intervene in the internal affairs of a sovereign state. If that duty is violated, the victim state has the further right to defend its territorial integrity and political independence. In the era of decolonization, the sovereign equality of states and the correlative norm of non-intervention received its most emphatic affirmation from the newly independent states.

2.9 At the same time, while intervention for human protection purposes was extremely rare, during the Cold War years state practice reflected the unwillingness of many countries to give up the use of intervention for political or other purposes as an instrument of policy. Leaders on both sides of the ideological divide intervened in support of friendly leaders against local populations, while also supporting rebel movements and other opposition causes in states to which they were ideologically opposed. None were prepared to rule out a priori the use of force in another country in order to rescue nationals who were trapped and threatened there.

2.10 The established and universally acknowledged right to self-defence, embodied in Article 51 of the UN Charter, was sometimes extended to include the right to launch punitive raids into neighbouring countries that had shown themselves unwilling or unable to stop their territory from being used as a launching pad for cross-border armed raids or terrorist attacks. But all that said, the many examples of intervention in actual state practice throughout the 20th century did not lead to an abandonment of the norm of non-intervention.

The Organizing Principle of the UN System

2.11 Membership of the United Nations was the final symbol of independent sovereign statehood and thus the seal of acceptance into the community of nations. The UN also became the principal international forum for collaborative action in the shared pursuit of the three goals of state building, nation building and economic development. The UN was therefore the main arena for the jealous protection, not the casual abrogation, of state sovereignty.

2.12 The UN is an organization dedicated to the maintenance of international peace and security on the basis of protecting the territorial integrity, political independence and national sovereignty of its member states. But the overwhelming majority of today's armed conflicts are internal, not inter-state. Moreover, the proportion of civilians killed in them increased from about one in ten at the start of the 20th century to around nine in ten by its close. This has presented the organization with a major difficulty: how to reconcile its foundational principles of member states' sovereignty and the accompanying primary mandate to maintain international peace and security ("to save succeeding generations from the scourge of war")—with the equally compelling mission to promote the interests and welfare of people within those states ("We the peoples of the United Nations").

2.13 The Secretary-General has discussed the dilemma in the conceptual language of two notions of sovereignty, one vesting in the state, the second in the people and in individuals. His approach reflects the ever-increasing commitment around the world to democratic government (of, by and for the people) and greater popular freedoms. The second notion of sovereignty to which he refers should not be seen as any kind of challenge to the traditional notion of state sovereignty. Rather it is a way of saying that the more traditional notion of state sovereignty should be able comfortably to embrace the goal of greater self-empowerment and freedom for people, both individually and collectively.

Sovereignty as Responsibility

2.14 The Charter of the UN is itself an example of an international obligation voluntarily accepted by member states. On the one hand, in granting membership of the UN, the international community welcomes the signatory state as a responsible member of the community of nations. On the other hand, the state itself, in signing the Charter, accepts the responsibilities of membership flowing from that signature. There is no transfer or dilution of state sovereignty. But there is a necessary recharacterization involved: from *sovereignty as control* to *sovereignty as responsibility* in both internal functions and external duties.

2.15 Thinking of sovereignty as responsibility, in a way that is being increasingly recognized in state practice, has a threefold significance. First, it implies that the state authorities are responsible for the functions of protecting the safety and lives of citizens and promotion of their welfare. Secondly, it suggests that the national political authorities are responsible to the citizens internally and to the international community through the UN. And thirdly, it means that the agents of state are responsible for their actions; that is to say, they are accountable for their acts of commission and omission. The case for thinking of sovereignty in these terms is strengthened by the ever-increasing impact of international human rights norms, and the increasing impact in international discourse of the concept of human security.

HUMAN RIGHTS, HUMAN SECURITY
AND EMERGING PRACTICE

Human Rights

2.16 The adoption of new standards of conduct for states in the protection and advancement of international human rights has been one of the great achievements of the post–World War II era. Article 1.3 of its founding 1945 Charter committed the UN to "promoting and encouraging respect for human rights and for fundamental freedoms for all without distinction as to race, sex, language or religion." The Universal Declaration of Human Rights (1948) embodies the moral code, political consensus and legal synthesis of human rights. The simplicity of the Declaration's language belies the passion of conviction underpinning it. Its elegance has been the font of inspiration down the decades; its provisions comprise the vocabulary of complaint. The two Covenants of 1966, on civil-political and social-economic-cultural rights, affirm and proclaim the human rights norm as a fundamental principle of international relations and add force and specificity to the Universal Declaration.

2.17 Together the Universal Declaration and the two Covenants mapped out the international human rights agenda, established the benchmark for state conduct, inspired provisions in many national laws and international conventions, and led to the creation of long-term national infrastructures for the protection and promotion of human rights. They are important milestones in the transition from a culture of violence to a more enlightened culture of peace.

2.18 What has been gradually emerging is a parallel transition from a culture of sovereign impunity to a culture of national and international accountability. International organizations, civil society activists and NGOs use the international human rights norms and instruments as the concrete point of reference against which to judge state conduct. Between them, the UN and NGOs have achieved many successes. National laws and international instruments have been improved, a number of political prisoners have been freed and some victims of abuse have been compensated. The most recent advances in international human rights have been in the further development of international humanitarian law, for example in the Ottawa Convention on landmines which subordinated military calculations to humanitarian concerns about a weapon that cannot distinguish a soldier from a child, and in the Rome Statute establishing the International Criminal Court.

2.19 Just as the substance of human rights law is coming increasingly closer to realizing the notion of universal justice—justice without borders—so too is the process. Not only have new international criminal tribunals been specially created to deal with crimes against humanity committed in the Balkans, Rwanda and Sierra Leone; and not only is an International Criminal Court about to be established to try such crimes wherever and whenever committed in the future; but, as already noted in Chapter 1, the universal jurisdiction which now exists under a number of treaties, like the Geneva Conventions, and which enables any state party to try anyone accused of the crimes in question, is now beginning to be seriously applied.

2.20 The significance of these developments in establishing new standards of behaviour, and new means of enforcing those standards, is unquestionable. But the key to the effective observance of human rights remains, as it always has been, national law and practice: the frontline defence of the rule of law is best conducted by the judicial systems of sovereign states, which should be independent, professional and properly resourced. It is only when national systems of justice either cannot or will not act to judge crimes against humanity that universal jurisdiction and other international options should come into play.

Human Security

2.21 The meaning and scope of security have become much broader since the UN Charter was signed in 1945. Human security means the security of people—their physical safety, their economic and social well-being, respect for their dignity and worth as human beings, and the protection of their human rights and fundamental freedoms. The growing recognition worldwide that concepts of security must include people as well as states has marked an important shift in international thinking during the past decade. Secretary-General Kofi Annan himself put the issue of human security at the centre of the current debate, when in his statement to the 54th session of the General Assembly he made clear his intention to "address the prospects for human security and intervention in the next century."

2.22 This Commission certainly accepts that issues of sovereignty and intervention are not just matters affecting the rights or prerogatives of states, but that they deeply affect and involve individual human beings in fundamental ways. One of the virtues of expressing the key issue in this debate as "the responsibility to protect" is that it focuses attention where it should be most concentrated, on the human needs of those seeking protection or assistance. The emphasis in the security debate shifts, with this focus, from territorial security, and security through armaments, to security through human development with access to food and employment, and to environmental security. The fundamental components of human security—the security of *people* against threats to life, health, livelihood, personal safety and human dignity—can be put at risk by external aggression, but also by factors within a country, including "security" forces. Being wedded still to too narrow a concept of "national security" may be one reason why many governments spend more to protect their citizens against undefined external military attack than to guard them against the omnipresent enemies of good health and other real threats to human security on a daily basis.

2.23 The traditional, narrow perception of security leaves out the most elementary and legitimate concerns of ordinary people regarding security in their daily lives. It also diverts enormous amounts of national wealth and human resources into armaments and armed forces, while countries fail to protect their citizens from chronic insecurities of hunger, disease, inadequate shelter, crime, unemployment, social conflict and environmental hazard. When rape is used as an instrument of war and ethnic cleansing, when thousands are killed by floods resulting from a ravaged countryside and when citizens are killed by their own security forces, then it is just insufficient to think of security in terms of national or territorial security alone. The concept of human security can and does embrace such diverse circumstances.

Emerging Practice

2.24 The debate on military intervention for human protection purposes was ignited in the international community essentially because of the critical gap between, on the one hand, the needs and distress being felt, and seen to be felt, in the real world, and on the other hand, the codified instruments and modalities for managing world order. There has been a parallel gap, no less critical, between the codified best practice of international behaviour as articulated in the UN Charter and actual state practice as it has evolved in the 56 years since the Charter was signed.

While there is not yet a sufficiently strong basis to claim the emergence of a new principle of customary international law, growing state and regional organization practice as well as Security Council precedent suggest an emerging guiding principle—which in the Commission's view could properly be termed "the responsibility to protect."

2.25 The emerging principle in question is that intervention for human protection purposes, including military intervention in extreme cases, is supportable when major harm to civilians is occurring or imminently apprehended, and the state in question is unable or unwilling to end the harm, or is itself the perpetrator. The Security Council itself has been increasingly prepared in recent years to act on this basis, most obviously in Somalia, defining what was essentially an internal situation as constituting a threat to international peace and security such as to justify enforcement action under Chapter VII of the UN Charter. This is also the basis on which the interventions by the Economic Community of West African States (ECOWAS) in Liberia and Sierra Leone were essentially justified by the interveners, as was the intervention mounted without Security Council authorization by NATO allies in Kosovo.

2.26 The notion that there is an emerging guiding principle in favour of military intervention for human protection purposes is also supported by a wide variety of legal sources—including sources that exist independently of any duties, responsibilities or authority that may be derived from Chapter VII of the UN Charter. These legal foundations include fundamental natural law principles; the human rights provisions of the UN Charter; the Universal Declaration of Human Rights together with the Genocide Convention; the Geneva Conventions and Additional Protocols on international humanitarian law; the statute of the International Criminal Court; and a number of other international human rights and human protection agreements and covenants. Some of the ramifications and consequences of these developments will be addressed again in Chapter 6 of this report as part of the examination of the question of authority.

2.27 Based on our reading of state practice, Security Council precedent, established norms, emerging guiding principles, and evolving customary international law, the Commission believes that the Charter's strong bias against military intervention is not to be regarded as absolute when decisive action is required on human protection grounds. The degree of legitimacy accorded to intervention will usually turn on the answers to such questions as the purpose, the means, the exhaustion of other avenues of redress against grievances, the proportionality of the riposte to the initiating provocation, and the agency of authorization. These are all questions that will recur: for present purposes the point is simply that there is a large and accumulating body of law and practice which supports the notion that, whatever form the exercise of that responsibility may properly take, members of the broad community of states do have a responsibility to protect both their own citizens and those of other states as well.

SHIFTING THE TERMS OF THE DEBATE

2.28 The traditional language of the sovereignty-intervention debate—in terms of "the right of humanitarian intervention" or the "right to intervene"—is unhelpful in at least three key respects. First, it necessarily focuses attention on the claims, rights and prerogatives of the potentially intervening states much more so than on the urgent needs of the potential beneficiaries of the action. Secondly, by focusing narrowly on the act of intervention, the traditional language does not adequately take into account the need for either prior [p]reventive effort or subsequent follow-up assistance, both of which have been too often neglected in practice. And thirdly, although this point should not be overstated, the familiar language does effectively operate to trump sovereignty with intervention at the outset of the debate: it loads the dice in favour of intervention before the argument has even begun, by tending to label and delegitimize dissent as anti-humanitarian.

2.29 The Commission is of the view that the debate about intervention for human protection purposes should focus not on "the right to intervene" but on "the responsibility to protect." The proposed change in terminology is also a change in perspective, reversing the perceptions inherent in the traditional language, and adding some additional ones:

—First, the responsibility to protect implies an evaluation of the issues from the point of view of those seeking or needing support, rather than those who may be considering intervention. Our preferred terminology refocuses the international searchlight back where it should always be: on the duty to protect communities from mass killing, women from systematic rape and children from starvation.

—Secondly, the responsibility to protect acknowledges that the primary responsibility in this regard rests with the state concerned, and that it is only if the state is unable or unwilling to fulfill this responsibility, or is itself the perpetrator, that it becomes the responsibility of the international community to act in its place. In many cases, the state will seek to acquit its responsibility in full and active partnership with representatives of the international community. Thus the "responsibility to protect" is more of a linking concept that bridges the divide between intervention and sovereignty; the language of the "right or duty to intervene" is intrinsically more confrontational.

—Thirdly, the responsibility to protect means not just the "responsibility to react," but the "responsibility to prevent" and the "responsibility to rebuild" as well. It directs our attention to the costs and results of action versus no action, and provides conceptual, normative and operational linkages between assistance, intervention and reconstruction.

2.30 The Commission believes that responsibility to protect resides first and foremost with the state whose people are directly affected. This fact reflects not only international law and the modern state system, also the practical realities of who is best placed to make a positive difference. The domestic authority is best placed to take action to prevent problems from turning into potential conflicts. When problems arise, the domestic authority is also best placed to understand them and to deal with them. When solutions are needed, it is the citizens of a particular state who have the greatest interest and the largest stake in the success of those solutions, in ensuring that the domestic authorities are fully accountable for their actions or inactions in addressing these problems, and in helping to ensure that past problems are not allowed to recur.

2.31 While the state whose people are directly affected has the default responsibility to protect, a residual responsibility also lies with the broader community of states. This fallback responsibility is activated when a particular state is clearly either unwilling or unable to fulfill its responsibility to protect or is itself the actual perpetrator of crimes or atrocities; or where people living outside a particular state are directly threatened by actions taking place there. This responsibility also requires that in some circumstances action must be taken by the broader community of states to support populations that are in jeopardy or under serious threat.

2.32 The substance of the responsibility to protect is the provision of life-supporting protection and assistance to populations at risk. This responsibility has three integral and essential components: not just the responsibility to *react* to an actual or apprehended human catastrophe, but the responsibility to *prevent* it, and the responsibility to *rebuild* after the event. Each of these will be dealt with in detail in chapters of this report. But it is important to emphasize from the start that action in support of the responsibility to protect necessarily involves and calls for a broad range and wide variety of assistance actions and responses. These actions may include both long- and short-term measures to help prevent human security-threatening situations from occurring, intensifying, spreading, or persisting; and rebuilding support to help prevent them from recurring; as well as, at least in extreme cases, military intervention to protect at-risk civilians from harm.

2.33 Changing the terms of the debate from "right to intervene" to "responsibility to protect" helps to shift the focus of discussion where it belongs—on the requirements of those who need or seek assistance. But while this is an important and necessary step, it does not by itself, as we have already acknowledged, resolve the difficult questions relating to the circumstances in which the responsibility to protect should be exercised—questions of legitimacy, authority, operational effectiveness and political will. These issues are fully addressed in subsequent chapters. While the Commission does not purport to try to resolve all of these difficult issues now and forever, our approach will hopefully generate innovative thinking on ways of achieving and sustaining effective and appropriate action.

Note

International Commission on Intervention and State Sovereignty, *The Responsibility to Protect*, December 2001 (www.iciss.ca/report2-en.asp).

Excerpts from the

National Security Strategy of the
United States of America (2002)

V. Prevent Our Enemies from Threatening Us, Our Allies, and Our Friends with Weapons of Mass Destruction

The gravest danger to freedom lies at the crossroads of radicalism and technology. When the spread of chemical and biological and nuclear weapons, along with ballistic missile technology—when that occurs, even weak states and small groups could attain a catastrophic power to strike great nations. Our enemies have declared this very intention, and have been caught seeking these terrible weapons. They want the capability to blackmail us, or to harm us, or to harm our friends—and we will oppose them with all our power.

President Bush, West Point, New York, June 1, 2002

The nature of the Cold War threat required the United States—with our allies and friends—to emphasize deterrence of the enemy's use of force, producing a grim strategy of mutual assured destruction. With the collapse of the Soviet Union and the end of the Cold War, our security environment has undergone profound transformation.

Having moved from confrontation to cooperation as the hallmark of our relationship with Russia, the dividends are evident: an end to the balance of terror that divided us; an historic reduction in the nuclear arsenals on both sides; and cooperation in areas such as counterterrorism and missile defense that until recently were inconceivable.

But new deadly challenges have emerged from rogue states and terrorists. None of these contemporary threats rival the sheer destructive power that was arrayed against us by the Soviet Union. However, the nature and motivations of these new adversaries, their determination to obtain destructive powers hitherto available only to the world's strongest states, and the greater likelihood that they will use weapons of mass destruction against us, make today's security environment more complex and dangerous.

In the 1990s we witnessed the emergence of a small number of rogue states that, while different in important ways, share a number of attributes. These states:

—brutalize their own people and squander their national resources for the personal gain of the rulers;

—display no regard for international law, threaten their neighbors, and callously violate international treaties to which they are party;

—are determined to acquire weapons of mass destruction, along with other advanced military technology, to be used as threats or offensively to achieve the aggressive designs of these regimes;

—sponsor terrorism around the globe; and

—reject basic human values and hate the United States and everything for which it stands.

At the time of the Gulf War, we acquired irrefutable proof that Iraq's designs were not limited to the chemical weapons it had used against Iran and its own people, but also extended to the acquisition of nuclear weapons and biological agents. In the past decade North Korea has become the world's principal purveyor of ballistic missiles, and has tested increasingly capable missiles while developing its own WMD arsenal. Other rogue regimes seek nuclear, biological, and chemical weapons as well. These states' pursuit of, and global trade in, such weapons has become a looming threat to all nations.

We must be prepared to stop rogue states and their terrorist clients before they are able to threaten or use weapons of mass destruction against the United States and our allies and friends. Our response must take full advantage of strengthened alliances, the establishment of new partnerships with former adversaries, innovation in the use of military forces, modern technologies, including the development of an effective missile defense system, and increased emphasis on intelligence collection and analysis.

Our comprehensive strategy to combat WMD includes:

—*Proactive counterproliferation efforts.* We must deter and defend against the threat before it is unleashed. We must ensure that key capabilities—detection, active and passive defenses, and counterforce capabilities—are integrated into our defense transformation and our homeland security systems. Counterproliferation must also be integrated into the doctrine, training, and equipping of our forces and those of our allies to ensure that we can prevail in any conflict with WMD-armed adversaries.

—*Strengthened nonproliferation efforts to prevent rogue states and terrorists from acquiring the materials, technologies, and expertise necessary for weapons of mass destruction.* We will enhance diplomacy, arms control, multilateral export controls, and threat reduction assistance that impede states and terrorists seeking WMD, and when necessary, interdict enabling technologies and materials. We will continue to build coalitions to support these efforts, encouraging their increased political and financial support for nonproliferation and threat reduction programs. The recent G-8 agreement to commit up to $20 billion to a global partnership against proliferation marks a major step forward.

—*Effective consequence management to respond to the effects of WMD use, whether by terrorists or hostile states.* Minimizing the effects of WMD use against our people will help deter those who possess such weapons and dissuade those who seek to acquire them by persuading enemies that they cannot attain their desired ends. The United States must also be prepared to respond to the effects of WMD use against our forces abroad, and to help friends and allies if they are attacked.

It has taken almost a decade for us to comprehend the true nature of this new threat. Given the goals of rogue states and terrorists, the United States can no longer solely rely on a reactive posture as we have in the past. The inability to deter a potential attacker, the immediacy of today's threats, and the magnitude of potential harm that could be caused by our adversaries' choice of weapons, do not permit that option. We cannot let our enemies strike first.

—In the Cold War, especially following the Cuban missile crisis, we faced a generally status quo, risk-averse adversary. Deterrence was an effective defense. But deterrence based only upon the threat of retaliation is less likely to work against leaders of rogue states more willing to take risks, gambling with the lives of their people, and the wealth of their nations.

—In the Cold War, weapons of mass destruction were considered weapons of last resort whose use risked the destruction of those who used them. Today, our enemies see weapons of mass destruction as weapons of choice. For rogue states these weapons are tools of intimidation and military aggression against their neighbors. These weapons may also allow these states to attempt to blackmail the United States and our allies to prevent us from deterring or repelling the aggressive behavior of rogue states. Such states also see these weapons as their best means of overcoming the conventional superiority of the United States.

—Traditional concepts of deterrence will not work against a terrorist enemy whose avowed tactics are wanton destruction and the targeting of innocents; whose so-called soldiers seek martyrdom in death and whose most potent protection is statelessness. The overlap between states that sponsor terror and those that pursue WMD compels us to action.

For centuries, international law recognized that nations need not suffer an attack before they can lawfully take action to defend themselves against forces that present an imminent danger of attack. Legal scholars and international jurists often conditioned the legitimacy of preemption on the existence of an imminent threat—most often a visible mobilization of armies, navies, and air forces preparing to attack.

We must adapt the concept of imminent threat to the capabilities and objectives of today's adversaries. Rogue states and terrorists do not seek to attack us using conventional means. They know such attacks would fail. Instead, they rely on acts of terror and, potentially, the use of weapons of mass destruction—weapons that can be easily concealed, delivered covertly, and used without warning.

The targets of these attacks are our military forces and our civilian population, in direct violation of one of the principal norms of the law of warfare. As was demonstrated by the losses on September 11, 2001, mass civilian casualties is the specific objective of terrorists and these losses would be exponentially more severe if terrorists acquired and used weapons of mass destruction.

The United States has long maintained the option of preemptive actions to counter a sufficient threat to our national security. The greater the threat, the greater is the risk of inaction—and the more compelling the case for taking anticipatory action to defend ourselves, even if uncertainty remains as to the time and place of the enemy's attack. To forestall or prevent such hostile acts by our adversaries, the United States will, if necessary, act preemptively.

The United States will not use force in all cases to preempt emerging threats, nor should nations use preemption as a pretext for aggression. Yet in an age where the enemies of civilization openly and actively seek the world's most destructive technologies, the United States cannot remain idle while dangers gather.

We will always proceed deliberately, weighing the consequences of our actions. To support preemptive options, we will:

—build better, more integrated intelligence capabilities to provide timely, accurate information on threats, wherever they may emerge;

—coordinate closely with allies to form a common assessment of the most dangerous threats; and

—continue to transform our military forces to ensure our ability to conduct rapid and precise operations to achieve decisive results.

The purpose of our actions will always be to eliminate a specific threat to the United States or our allies and friends. The reasons for our actions will be clear, the force measured, and the cause just.

Note

White House, *The National Security Strategy of the United States of America,* September 2002 (www.whitehouse.gov/nsc/nss.pdf).

Excerpts from the

Report of the UN Secretary–General's High-level
Panel on Threats, Challenges and Change (2005)

Part 3: Collective security and the use of force

IX. USING FORCE: RULES AND GUIDELINES

183. The framers of the Charter of the United Nations recognized that force may be necessary for the "prevention and removal of threats to the peace, and for the suppression of acts of aggression or other breaches of the peace." Military force, legally and properly applied, is a vital component of any workable system of collective security, whether defined in the traditional narrow sense or more broadly as we would prefer. But few contemporary policy issues cause more difficulty, or involve higher stakes, than the principles concerning its use and application to individual cases.

184. The maintenance of world peace and security depends importantly on there being a common global understanding, and acceptance, of when the application of force is both legal and legitimate. One of these elements being satisfied without the other will always weaken the international legal order—and thereby put both State and human security at greater risk.

A. The question of legality

185. The Charter of the United Nations, in Article 2.4, expressly prohibits Member States from using or threatening force against each other,

allowing only two exceptions: self-defence under Article 51, and military measures authorized by the Security Council under Chapter VII (and by extension for regional organizations under Chapter VIII) in response to "any threat to the peace, breach of the peace or act of aggression."

186. For the first 44 years of the United Nations, Member States often violated these rules and used military force literally hundreds of times, with a paralysed Security Council passing very few Chapter VII resolutions and Article 51 only rarely providing credible cover. Since the end of the cold war, however, the yearning for an international system governed by the rule of law has grown. There is little evident international acceptance of the idea of security being best preserved by a balance of power, or by any single—even benignly motivated—superpower.

187. But in seeking to apply the express language of the Charter, three particularly difficult questions arise in practice: first, when a State claims the right to strike preventively, in self-defence, in response to a threat which is not imminent; secondly, when a State appears to be posing an external threat, actual or potential, to other States or people outside its borders, but there is disagreement in the Security Council as to what to do about it; and thirdly, where the threat is primarily internal, to a State's own people.

1. Article 51 of the Charter of the United Nations and self-defence

188. The language of this article is restrictive: "Nothing in the present Charter shall impair the inherent right of individual or collective self-defense if an armed attack occurs against a member of the United Nations, until the Security Council has taken measures to maintain international peace and security." However, a threatened State, according to long established international law, can take military action as long as the threatened attack is *imminent*, no other means would deflect it and the action is proportionate. The problem arises where the threat in question is not imminent but still claimed to be real: for example the acquisition, with allegedly hostile intent, of nuclear weapons-making capability.

189. Can a State, without going to the Security Council, claim in these circumstances the right to act, in anticipatory self-defence, not just pre-emptively (against an imminent or proximate threat) but preventively (against a non-imminent or non-proximate one)? Those who say "yes" argue that the potential harm from some threats (e.g., terrorists armed with a nuclear weapon) is so great that one simply cannot risk waiting

until they become imminent, and that less harm may be done (e.g., avoiding a nuclear exchange or radioactive fallout from a reactor destruction) by acting earlier.

190. The short answer is that if there are good arguments for preventive military action, with good evidence to support them, they should be put to the Security Council, which can authorize such action if it chooses to. If it does not so choose, there will be, by definition, time to pursue other strategies, including persuasion, negotiation, deterrence and containment—and to visit again the military option.

191. For those impatient with such a response, the answer must be that, in a world full of perceived potential threats, the risk to the global order and the norm of non-intervention on which it continues to be based is simply too great for the legality of unilateral preventive action, as distinct from collectively endorsed action, to be accepted. Allowing one to so act is to allow all.

192. **We do not favour the rewriting or reinterpretation of Article 51.**

2. Chapter VII of the Charter of the United Nations and external threats

193. In the case of a State posing a threat to other States, people outside its borders or to international order more generally, the language of Chapter VII is inherently broad enough, and has been interpreted broadly enough, to allow the Security Council to approve any coercive action at all, including military action, against a State when it deems this "necessary to maintain or restore international peace and security." That is the case whether the threat is occurring now, in the imminent future or more distant future; whether it involves the State's own actions or those of non-State actors it harbours or supports; or whether it takes the form of an act or omission, an actual or potential act of violence or simply a challenge to the Council's authority.

194. We emphasize that the concerns we expressed about the legality of the preventive use of military force in the case of self-defence under Article 51 are not applicable in the case of collective action authorized under Chapter VII. In the world of the twenty-first century, the international community does have to be concerned about nightmare scenarios combining terrorists, weapons of mass destruction and irresponsible States, and much more besides, which may conceivably justify the use of force, not just reactively but preventively and before a latent threat becomes imminent. The question is not whether such action can be taken:

it can, by the Security Council as the international community's collective security voice, at any time it deems that there is a threat to international peace and security. The Council may well need to be prepared to be much more proactive on these issues, taking more decisive action earlier, than it has been in the past.

195. Questions of legality apart, there will be issues of prudence, or legitimacy, about whether such preventive action *should* be taken: crucial among them is whether there is credible evidence of the reality of the threat in question (taking into account both capability and specific intent) and whether the military response is the only reasonable one in the circumstances. We address these issues further below.

196. It may be that some States will always feel that they have the obligation to their own citizens, and the capacity, to do whatever they feel they need to do, unburdened by the constraints of [the] collective Security Council process. But however understandable that approach may have been in the cold war years, when the United Nations was manifestly not operating as an effective collective security system, the world has now changed and expectations about legal compliance are very much higher.

197. One of the reasons why States may want to bypass the Security Council is a lack of confidence in the quality and objectivity of its decision-making. The Council's decisions have often been less than consistent, less than persuasive and less than fully responsive to very real State and human security needs. But the solution is not to reduce the Council to impotence and irrelevance: it is to work from within to reform it, including in the ways we propose in the present report.

198. **The Security Council is fully empowered under Chapter VII of the Charter of the United Nations to address the full range of security threats with which States are concerned. The task is not to find alternatives to the Security Council as a source of authority but to make the Council work better than it has.**

3. Chapter VII of the Charter of the United Nations, internal threats and the responsibility to protect

199. The Charter of the United Nations is not as clear as it could be when it comes to saving lives within countries in situations of mass atrocity. It "reaffirm(s) faith in fundamental human rights" but does not do much to protect them, and Article 2.7 prohibits intervention "in matters which are essentially within the jurisdiction of any State." There has been,

as a result, a long-standing argument in the international community between those who insist on a "right to intervene" in man-made catastrophes and those who argue that the Security Council, for all its powers under Chapter VII to "maintain or restore international security," is prohibited from authorizing any coercive action against sovereign States for whatever happens within their borders.

200. Under the Convention on the Prevention and Punishment of the Crime of Genocide (Genocide Convention), States have agreed that genocide, whether committed in time of peace or in time of war, is a crime under international law which they undertake to prevent and punish. Since then it has been understood that genocide anywhere is a threat to the security of all and should never be tolerated. The principle of non-intervention in internal affairs cannot be used to protect genocidal acts or other atrocities, such as large-scale violations of international humanitarian law or large-scale ethnic cleansing, which can properly be considered a threat to international security and as such provoke action by the Security Council.

201. The successive humanitarian disasters in Somalia, Bosnia and Herzegovina, Rwanda, Kosovo and now Darfur, Sudan, have concentrated attention not on the immunities of sovereign Governments but their responsibilities, both to their own people and to the wider international community. There is a growing recognition that the issue is not the "right to intervene" of any State, but the "responsibility to protect" of *every* State when it comes to people suffering from avoidable catastrophe—mass murder and rape, ethnic cleansing by forcible expulsion and terror, and deliberate starvation and exposure to disease. And there is a growing acceptance that while sovereign Governments have the primary responsibility to protect their own citizens from such catastrophes, when they are unable or unwilling to do so that responsibility should be taken up by the wider international community—with it spanning a continuum involving prevention, response to violence, if necessary, and rebuilding shattered societies. The primary focus should be on assisting the cessation of violence through mediation and other tools and the protection of people through such measures as the dispatch of humanitarian, human rights and police missions. Force, if it needs to be used, should be deployed as a last resort.

202. The Security Council so far has been neither very consistent nor very effective in dealing with these cases, very often acting too late, too

hesitantly or not at all. But step by step, the Council and the wider international community have come to accept that, under Chapter VII and in pursuit of the emerging norm of a collective international responsibility to protect, it can always authorize military action to redress catastrophic internal wrongs if it is prepared to declare that the situation is a "threat to international peace and security," not especially difficult when breaches of international law are involved.

203. **We endorse the emerging norm that there is a collective international responsibility to protect, exercisable by the Security Council authorizing military intervention as a last resort, in the event of genocide and other large-scale killing, ethnic cleansing or serious violations of international humanitarian law which sovereign Governments have proved powerless or unwilling to prevent.**

B. The question of legitimacy

204. The effectiveness of the global collective security system, as with any other legal order, depends ultimately not only on the legality of decisions but also on the common perception of their legitimacy—their being made on solid evidentiary grounds, and for the right reasons, morally as well as legally.

205. If the Security Council is to win the respect it must have as the primary body in the collective security system, it is critical that its most important and influential decisions, those with large-scale life-and-death impact, be better made, better substantiated and better communicated. In particular, in deciding whether or not to authorize the use of force, the Council should adopt and systematically address a set of agreed guidelines, going directly not to whether force *can* legally be used but whether, as a matter of good conscience and good sense, it *should* be.

206. The guidelines we propose will not produce agreed conclusions with push-button predictability. The point of adopting them is not to guarantee that the objectively best outcome will always prevail. It is rather to maximize the possibility of achieving Security Council consensus around when it is appropriate or not to use coercive action, including armed force; to maximize international support for whatever the Security Council decides; and to minimize the possibility of individual Member States bypassing the Security Council.

207. **In considering whether to authorize or endorse the use of military force, the Security Council should always address—whatever other**

considerations it may take into account—at least the following five basic criteria of legitimacy:

(a) *Seriousness of threat.* Is the threatened harm to State or human security of a kind, and sufficiently clear and serious, to justify prima facie the use of military force? In the case of internal threats, does it involve genocide and other large-scale killing, ethnic cleansing or serious violations of international humanitarian law, actual or imminently apprehended?

(b) **Proper purpose.** Is it clear that the primary purpose of the proposed military action is to halt or avert the threat in question, whatever other purposes or motives may be involved?

(c) **Last resort.** Has every non-military option for meeting the threat in question been explored, with reasonable grounds for believing that other measures will not succeed?

(d) **Proportional means.** Are the scale, duration and intensity of the proposed military action the minimum necessary to meet the threat in question?

(e) **Balance of consequences.** Is there a reasonable chance of the military action being successful in meeting the threat in question, with the consequences of action not likely to be worse than the consequences of inaction?

208. **The above guidelines for authorizing the use of force should be embodied in declaratory resolutions of the Security Council and General Assembly.**

209. We also believe it would be valuable if individual Member States, whether or not they are members of the Security Council, subscribed to them.

X. PEACE ENFORCEMENT AND PEACEKEEPING CAPABILITY

210. When the Security Council makes a determination that force must be authorized, questions remain about the capacities at its disposal to implement that decision. In recent years, decisions to authorize military force for the purpose of enforcing the peace have primarily fallen to multinational forces. Blue helmet peacekeepers—in United Nations uniform and under direct United Nations command—have more frequently been deployed when forces are authorized with the consent of the parties to conflict, to help implement a peace agreement or monitor ceasefire lines after combat.

211. Discussion of the necessary capacities has been confused by the tendency to refer to peacekeeping missions as "Chapter VI operations" and peace enforcement missions as "Chapter VII operations"—meaning consent-based or coercion-based, respectively. This shorthand is also often used to distinguish missions that do not involve the use of deadly force for purposes other than self-defence, and those that do.

212. Both characterizations are to some extent misleading. There is a distinction between operations in which the robust use of force is integral to the mission from the outset (e.g., responses to cross-border invasions or an explosion of violence, in which the recent practice has been to mandate multinational forces) and operations in which there is a reasonable expectation that force may not be needed at all (e.g., traditional peacekeeping missions monitoring and verifying a ceasefire or those assisting in implementing peace agreements, where blue helmets are still the norm).

213. But both kinds of operation need the authorization of the Security Council (Article 51 self-defence cases apart), and in peacekeeping cases as much as in peace-enforcement cases it is now the usual practice for a Chapter VII mandate to be given (even if that is not always welcomed by troop contributors). This is on the basis that even the most benign environment can turn sour—when spoilers emerge to undermine a peace agreement and put civilians at risk—and that it is desirable for there to be complete certainty about the mission's capacity to respond with force, if necessary. On the other hand, the difference between Chapter VI and VII mandates can be exaggerated: there is little doubt that peacekeeping missions operating under Chapter VI (and thus operating without enforcement powers) have the right to use force in self-defence—and this right is widely understood to extend to "defence of the mission."

214. The real challenge, in any deployment of forces of any configuration with any role, is to ensure that they have (a) an appropriate, clear and well understood mandate, applicable to all the changing circumstances that might reasonably be envisaged, and (b) all the necessary resources to implement that mandate fully.

215. The demand for personnel for both full-scale peace-enforcement missions and peacekeeping missions remains higher than the ready supply. At the end of 2004, there are more than 60,000 peacekeepers deployed in 16 missions around the world. If international efforts stay on track to end several long-standing wars in Africa, the numbers of peacekeepers needed will soon substantially increase. In the absence of a commensurate increase

in available personnel, United Nations peacekeeping risks repeating some of its worst failures of the 1990s.

216. At present, the total global supply of personnel is constrained both by the fact that the armed forces of many countries remain configured for cold war duties, with less than 10 per cent of those in uniform available for active deployment at any given time, and by the fact that few nations have sufficient transport and logistic capabilities to move and supply those who are available. For peacekeeping, and in extreme cases peace enforcement, to continue to be an effective and accepted instrument of collective security, the availability of peacekeepers must grow. **The developed States have particular responsibilities here, and should do more to transform their existing force capacities into suitable contingents for peace operations.**

217. Prompt and effective response to today's challenges requires a dependable capacity for the rapid deployment of personnel and equipment for peacekeeping and law enforcement. States that have either global or regional air- or sea-lift capacities should make these available to the United Nations, either free of charge or on the basis of a negotiated fee-based structure for the reimbursement of the additional costs associated with United Nations use of these capacities.

218. **Member States should strongly support the efforts of the Department of Peacekeeping Operations of the United Nations Secretariat, building on the important work of the Panel on United Nations Peace Operations (see A/55/305-S/2000/809), to improve its use of strategic deployment stockpiles, standby arrangements, trust funds and other mechanisms to meet the tighter deadlines necessary for effective deployment.**

219. However, it is unlikely that the demand for rapid action will be met through United Nations mechanisms alone. We welcome the European Union decision to establish standby high readiness, self-sufficient battalions that can reinforce United Nations missions. **Others with advanced military capacities should be encouraged to develop similar capacities at up to brigade level and to place them at the disposal of the United Nations.**

(...)

XII. PROTECTING CIVILIANS

231. In many civil wars, combatants target civilians and relief workers with impunity. Beyond direct violence, deaths from starvation, disease

and the collapse of public health dwarf the numbers killed by bullets and bombs. Millions more are displaced internally or across borders. Human rights abuses and gender violence are rampant.

232. Under international law, the primary responsibility to protect civilians from suffering in war lies with belligerents—State or non-State. International humanitarian law provides minimum protection and standards applicable to the most vulnerable in situations of armed conflict, including women, children and refugees, and must be respected.

233. **All combatants must abide by the provisions of the Geneva Conventions. All Member States should sign, ratify and act on all treaties relating to the protection of civilians, such as the Genocide Convention, the Geneva Conventions, the Rome Statute of the International Criminal Court and all refugee conventions.**

234. Humanitarian aid is a vital tool for helping Governments to fulfil this responsibility. Its core purpose is to protect civilian victims, minimize their suffering and keep them alive during the conflict so that when war ends they have the opportunity to rebuild shattered lives. The provision of assistance is a necessary part of this effort. Donors must fully and equitably fund humanitarian protection and assistance operations.

235. The Secretary-General, based in part on work undertaken by the United Nations High Commissioner for Refugees and strong advocacy efforts by nongovernmental organizations, has prepared a 10-point platform for action for the protection of civilians in armed conflict. The Secretary-General's 10-point platform for action should be considered by all actors—States, NGOs and international organizations—in their efforts to protect civilians in armed conflict.

236. From this platform, particular attention should be placed on the question of access to civilians, which is routinely and often flagrantly denied. United Nations humanitarian field staff, as well as United Nations political and peacekeeping representatives, should be well trained and well supported to negotiate access. Such efforts also require better coordination of bilateral initiatives. The Security Council can use field missions and other diplomatic measures to enhance access to and protection of civilians.

237. Particularly egregious violations, such as occur when armed groups militarize refugee camps, require emphatic responses from the international community, including from the Security Council acting under Chapter VII of the Charter of the United Nations. Although the

Security Council has acknowledged that such militarization is a threat to peace and security, it has not developed the capacity or shown the will to confront the problem. **The Security Council should fully implement resolution 1265 (1999) on the protection of civilians in armed conflict.**

238. Of special concern is the use of sexual violence as a weapon of conflict. The human rights components of peacekeeping operations should be given explicit mandates and sufficient resources to investigate and report on human rights violations against women. Security Council resolution 1325 (2000) on women, peace and security and the associated Independent Experts' Assessment provide important additional recommendations for the protection of women. **The Security Council, United Nations agencies and Member States should fully implement its recommendations.**

Note

High-Level Panel on Threats, Challenges and Change, *A More Secure World: Our Shared Responsibility,* 2004 (www.un.org/secureworld/report3.pdf), notes omitted.

Excerpts from

In Larger Freedom: Towards Development, Security and Human Rights for All (2005)

III. Freedom from fear

(...)

E. USE OF FORCE

122. Finally, an essential part of the consensus we seek must be agreement on when and how force can be used to defend international peace and security. In recent years, this issue has deeply divided Member States. They have disagreed about whether States have the right to use military force pre-emptively, to defend themselves against imminent threats; whether they have the right to use it preventively to defend themselves against latent or non-imminent threats; and whether they have the right—or perhaps the obligation—to use it protectively to rescue the citizens of other States from genocide or comparable crimes.

123. Agreement must be reached on these questions if the United Nations is to be—as it was intended to be—a forum for resolving differences rather than a mere stage for acting them out. And yet I believe the Charter of our Organization, as it stands, offers a good basis for the understanding that we need.

124. Imminent threats are fully covered by Article 51, which safeguards the inherent right of sovereign States to defend themselves against

armed attack. Lawyers have long recognized that this covers an imminent attack as well as one that has already happened.

125. Where threats are not imminent but latent, the Charter gives full authority to the Security Council to use military force, including preventively, to preserve international peace and security. As to genocide, ethnic cleansing and other such crimes against humanity, are they not also threats to international peace and security, against which humanity should be able to look to the Security Council for protection?

126. The task is not to find alternatives to the Security Council as a source of authority but to make it work better. When considering whether to authorize or endorse the use of military force, the Council should come to a common view on how to weigh the seriousness of the threat; the proper purpose of the proposed military action; whether means short of the use of force might plausibly succeed in stopping the threat; whether the military option is proportional to the threat at hand; and whether there is a reasonable chance of success. By undertaking to make the case for military action in this way, the Council would add transparency to its deliberations and make its decisions more likely to be respected, by both Governments and world public opinion. **I therefore recommend that the Security Council adopt a resolution setting out these principles and expressing its intention to be guided by them when deciding whether to authorize or mandate the use of force.**

Note

United Nations, *In Larger Freedom: Towards Development, Security and Human Rights for All,* Report of the Secretary-General, March 2005 (www.un.org/largerfreedom/contents.htm).

Excerpts from the
National Security Strategy of the United States of America (2006)

V. Prevent Our Enemies from Threatening Us, Our Allies, and Our Friends with Weapons of Mass Destruction

A. SUMMARY OF NATIONAL SECURITY STRATEGY 2002

The security environment confronting the United States today is radically different from what we have faced before. Yet the first duty of the United States Government remains what it always has been: to protect the American people and American interests. It is an enduring American principle that this duty obligates the government to anticipate and counter threats, using all elements of national power, before the threats can do grave damage. The greater the threat, the greater is the risk of inaction—and the more compelling the case for taking anticipatory action to defend ourselves, even if uncertainty remains as to the time and place of the enemy's attack. There are few greater threats than a terrorist attack with WMD.

To forestall or prevent such hostile acts by our adversaries, the United States will, if necessary, act preemptively in exercising our inherent right of self-defense. The United States will not resort to force in all cases to preempt emerging threats. Our preference is that nonmilitary actions succeed. And no country should ever use preemption as a pretext for aggression.

Countering proliferation of WMD requires a comprehensive strategy involving strengthened nonproliferation efforts to deny these weapons of terror and related expertise to those seeking them; *proactive counterproliferation efforts* to defend against and defeat WMD and missile threats before they are unleashed; and *improved protection* to mitigate the consequences of WMD use. We aim to convince our adversaries that they cannot achieve their goals with WMD, and thus deter and dissuade them from attempting to use or even acquire these weapons in the first place.

B. CURRENT CONTEXT: SUCCESSES AND CHALLENGES

We have worked hard to protect our citizens and our security. The United States has worked extensively with the international community and key partners to achieve common objectives.

—The United States has begun fielding ballistic missile defenses to deter and protect the United States from missile attacks by rogue states armed with WMD. The fielding of such missile defenses was made possible by the United States' withdrawal from the 1972 Anti-Ballistic Missile Treaty, which was done in accordance with the treaty's provisions.

—In May 2003, the Administration launched the Proliferation Security Initiative (PSI), a global effort that aims to stop shipments of WMD, their delivery systems, and related material. More than 70 countries have expressed support for this initiative, and it has enjoyed several successes in impeding WMD trafficking.

—United States leadership in extensive law enforcement and intelligence cooperation involving several countries led to the roll-up of the A.Q. Khan nuclear network.

—Libya voluntarily agreed to eliminate its WMD programs shortly after a PSI interdiction of a shipment of nuclear-related material from the A.Q. Khan network to Libya.

—The United States led in securing passage in April 2004 of United Nations Security Council (UNSC) Resolution 1540, requiring nations to criminalize WMD proliferation and institute effective export and financial controls.

—We have led the effort to strengthen the ability of the International Atomic Energy Agency (IAEA) to detect and respond to nuclear proliferation.

—The Administration has established a new comprehensive framework, *Biodefense for the 21st Century*, incorporating innovative initiatives to protect the United States against bioterrorism.

Nevertheless, serious challenges remain:

—Iran has violated its Non-Proliferation Treaty safeguards obligations and refuses to provide objective guarantees that its nuclear program is solely for peaceful purposes.

—The DPRK continues to destabilize its region and defy the international community, now boasting a small nuclear arsenal and an illicit nuclear program in violation of its international obligations.

—Terrorists, including those associated with the al-Qaida network, continue to pursue WMD.

—Some of the world's supply of weapons-grade fissile material— the necessary ingredient for making nuclear weapons—is not properly protected.

—Advances in biotechnology provide greater opportunities for state and non-state actors to obtain dangerous pathogens and equipment.

C. THE WAY AHEAD

We are committed to keeping the world's most dangerous weapons out of the hands of the world's most dangerous people.

1. Nuclear Proliferation

The proliferation of nuclear weapons poses the greatest threat to our national security. Nuclear weapons are unique in their capacity to inflict instant loss of life on a massive scale. For this reason, nuclear weapons hold special appeal to rogue states and terrorists.

The best way to block aspiring nuclear states or nuclear terrorists is to deny them access to the essential ingredient of fissile material. It is much harder to deny states or terrorists other key components, for nuclear weapons represent a 60-year old technology and the knowledge is widespread. Therefore, our strategy focuses on controlling fissile material with two priority objectives: first, to keep states from acquiring the capability to produce fissile material suitable for making nuclear weapons; and second, to deter, interdict, or prevent any transfer of that material from states that have this capability to rogue states or to terrorists.

The first objective requires closing a loophole in the Non-Proliferation Treaty that permits regimes to produce fissile material that can be used to make nuclear weapons under cover of a civilian nuclear power program. To close this loophole, we have proposed that the world's leading nuclear exporters create a safe, orderly system that spreads nuclear energy without spreading nuclear weapons. Under this system, all states would have reliable access at reasonable cost to fuel for civilian nuclear power reactors. In return, those states would remain transparent and renounce the enrichment and reprocessing capabilities that can produce fissile material for nuclear weapons. In this way, enrichment and reprocessing will not be necessary for nations seeking to harness nuclear energy for strictly peaceful purposes.

The Administration has worked with the international community in confronting nuclear proliferation.

We may face no greater challenge from a single country than from Iran. For almost 20 years, the Iranian regime hid many of its key nuclear efforts from the international community. Yet the regime continues to claim that it does not seek to develop nuclear weapons. The Iranian regime's true intentions are clearly revealed by the regime's refusal to negotiate in good faith; its refusal to come into compliance with its international obligations by providing the IAEA access to nuclear sites and resolving troubling questions; and the aggressive statements of its President calling for Israel to "be wiped off the face of the earth." The United States has joined with our EU partners and Russia to pressure Iran to meet its international obligations and provide objective guarantees that its nuclear program is only for peaceful purposes. This diplomatic effort must succeed if confrontation is to be avoided.

As important as are these nuclear issues, the United States has broader concerns regarding Iran. The Iranian regime sponsors terrorism; threatens Israel; seeks to thwart Middle East peace; disrupts democracy in Iraq; and denies the aspirations of its people for freedom. The nuclear issue and our other concerns can ultimately be resolved only if the Iranian regime makes the strategic decision to change these policies, open up its political system, and afford freedom to its people. This is the ultimate goal of U.S. policy. In the interim, we will continue to take all necessary measures to protect our national and economic security against the adverse effects of their bad conduct. The problems lie with the illicit behavior and dangerous ambition of the Iranian regime, not the legitimate aspirations and interests of the Iranian people. Our strategy is to block the threats posed by the regime while expanding our engagement and outreach to the people the regime is oppressing.

The North Korean regime also poses a serious nuclear proliferation challenge. It presents a long and bleak record of duplicity and bad-faith negotiations. In the past, the regime has attempted to split the United

States from its allies. This time, the United States has successfully forged a consensus among key regional partners—China, Japan, Russia, and the Republic of Korea (ROK)—that the DPRK must give up all of its existing nuclear programs. Regional cooperation offers the best hope for a peaceful, diplomatic resolution of this problem. In a joint statement signed on September 19, 2005, in the Six-Party Talks among these participants, the DPRK agreed to abandon its nuclear weapons and all existing nuclear programs. The joint statement also declared that the relevant parties would negotiate a permanent peace for the Korean peninsula and explore ways to promote security cooperation in Asia. Along with our partners in the Six-Party Talks, the United States will continue to press the DPRK to implement these commitments.

The United States has broader concerns regarding the DPRK as well. The DPRK counterfeits our currency; traffics in narcotics and engages in other illicit activities; threatens the ROK with its army and its neighbors with its missiles; and brutalizes and starves its people. The DPRK regime needs to change these policies, open up its political system, and afford freedom to its people. In the interim, we will continue to take all necessary measures to protect our national and economic security against the adverse effects of their bad conduct.

The second nuclear proliferation objective is to keep fissile material out of the hands of rogue states and terrorists. To do this we must address the danger posed by inadequately safeguarded nuclear and radiological materials worldwide. The Administration is leading a global effort to reduce and secure such materials as quickly as possible through several initiatives including the Global Threat Reduction Initiative (GTRI). The GTRI locates, tracks, and reduces existing stockpiles of nuclear material. This new initiative also discourages trafficking in nuclear material by emplacing detection equipment at key transport nodes.

Building on the success of the PSI, the United States is also leading international efforts to shut down WMD trafficking by targeting key maritime and air transportation and transshipment routes, and by cutting off proliferators from financial resources that support their activities.

2. Biological Weapons
Biological weapons also pose a grave WMD threat because of the risks of contagion that would spread disease across large populations and around the globe. Unlike nuclear weapons, biological weapons do not require

hard-to-acquire infrastructure or materials. This makes the challenge of controlling their spread even greater.

Countering the spread of biological weapons requires a strategy focused on improving our capacity to detect and respond to biological attacks, securing dangerous pathogens, and limiting the spread of materials useful for biological weapons. The United States is working with partner nations and institutions to strengthen global biosurveillance capabilities for early detection of suspicious outbreaks of disease. We have launched new initiatives at home to modernize our public health infrastructure and to encourage industry to speed the development of new classes of vaccines and medical countermeasures. This will also enhance our Nation's ability to respond to pandemic public health threats, such as avian influenza.

3. Chemical Weapons

Chemical weapons are a serious proliferation concern and are actively sought by terrorists, including al-Qaida. Much like biological weapons, the threat from chemical weapons increases with advances in technology, improvements in agent development, and ease in acquisition of materials and equipment.

To deter and defend against such threats, we work to identify and disrupt terrorist networks that seek chemical weapons capabilities, and seek to deny them access to materials needed to make these weapons. We are improving our detection and other chemical defense capabilities at home and abroad, including ensuring that U.S. military forces and emergency responders are trained and equipped to manage the consequences of a chemical weapons attack.

4. The Need for Action

The new strategic environment requires new approaches to deterrence and defense. Our deterrence strategy no longer rests primarily on the grim premise of inflicting devastating consequences on potential foes. Both offenses and defenses are necessary to deter state and non-state actors, through denial of the objectives of their attacks and, if necessary, responding with overwhelming force.

Safe, credible, and reliable nuclear forces continue to play a critical role. We are strengthening deterrence by developing a New Triad composed of offensive strike systems (both nuclear and improved conventional capabilities); active and passive defenses, including missile defenses; and a responsive infrastructure, all bound together by enhanced command and control, planning, and intelligence systems. These capabilities will better deter some of the new threats we face, while also bolstering our security commitments to allies. Such security commitments have played a crucial role in convincing some countries to forgo their own nuclear weapons programs, thereby aiding our nonproliferation objectives.

Deterring potential foes and assuring friends and allies, however, is only part of a broader approach. Meeting WMD proliferation challenges also requires effective international action—and the international community is most engaged in such action when the United States leads.

Taking action need not involve military force. Our strong preference and common practice is to address proliferation concerns through international diplomacy, in concert with key allies and regional partners. If necessary, however, under long-standing principles of self defense, we do not rule out the use of force before attacks occur, even if uncertainty remains as to the time and place of the enemy's attack. When the consequences of an attack with WMD are potentially so devastating, we cannot afford to stand idly by as grave dangers materialize. This is the principle and logic of preemption. The place of preemption in our national security strategy remains the same. We will always proceed deliberately, weighing the consequences of our actions. The reasons for our actions will be clear, the force measured, and the cause just.

Note

White House, *National Security Strategy of the United States of America*, March 2006 (www.whitehouse.gov/nsc/nss/2006/nss2006.pdf).

Contributors

Ivo H. Daalder
Brookings Institution

Bruce W. Jentleson
Duke University

Anne E. Kramer
*Office of Congressman
Stephen Lynch*

Andrew J. Loomis
Georgetown University

Susan E. Rice
Brookings Institution

James B. Steinberg
University of Texas–Austin

Index

Abe, Shinzo (prime minister; Japan), 6
Abu Ghraib (prison in Iraq; U.S.), 45, 53
Afghanistan war (*2001*–present): goals, effects, and questions of, 10; invasion of, 25, 42; Northern Alliance and, 51–52; problems of, 41, 49–50; Soviet Union and, 48; Taliban and, 42, 49–50, 51, 52–53, 101, 102, 105; UN and, 10; U.S. and, *52–53*, 101, 102, 105; use of force and, 42–43, 99, 102, 105
Africa and Africans: military capacity in, 85–86, 89; responsibility to protect and, 123; views of NPT, 35; views of regional organizations, 121–22, 129; views of terrorism, 101, 103; views of UN, 123; views of use of military force, 3, 119. *See also* Horn of Africa; *individual countries*
African Union (AU): Burundi and, 88; capacity of, 81, 82, 129; charter of, 86, 119; Darfur and, 81, 91, 126; role of, 121–22; Somalia and, 44
Aggression, 20–21. *See also* Military force; War

Agreed Framework (U.S.-North Korea; *1994*), 24, 29–30, 113
Ahmadinejad, Mahmoud (president; Iran), 109. *See also* Iran
Aideed, Mohammed (warlord; Somalia), 69
Albania and Albanians, 1, 10, 74, 78–79, 119
Albright, Madeleine (UN ambassador; U.S.), 77
Algeria, 48
Al Qaeda: in Afghanistan, 10, 49, 50, 51–53; bases of, 48; Hussein, Saddam and, 46; in Madrid, 44; in Somalia, 46; strategy of, 48; transformation of, 50, 103; in Yemen, 42
Amin, Idi (president; Uganda), 61
Amnesty International, 61
Annan, Kofi (secretary general; UN): definition of terrorism, 100–01; High-Level Panel and, 4, 8; humanitarian intervention and, 80; preemption and, 7; responsibility to protect and, 118; Rwanda and, 72; Security Council and, 9, 84, 128
Arab League, 87